Enjoy the read.
This stuff works!

BRANDING IS OUT, RESULTS ARE IN!

LESSONS FOR THE <u>LOCAL</u> ADVERTISER

TOM RAY

BRANDING IS OUT, RESULTS ARE IN!

LESSONS FOR THE <u>LOCAL</u> ADVERTISER

Jim Doyle & Associates
7711 Holiday Drive
Sarasota, FL 34231

(941) 926-7355
FAX: (941) 925-1114
Tom@jimdoyle.com
www.jimdoyle.com
www.doyleondemand.com

This book is dedicated to Main St., USA, the LOCAL businesses that make our lives better and our economy hum.

CONTENTS

ACKNOWLEDGEMENTS

In 2005, at a particularly unfulfilling time in my career, I was introduced to Jim Doyle. A mutual friend made the connection and I will be forever grateful. I joined Jim Doyle & Associates and have loved every minute since. Not only is Jim a brilliant marketer and mentor, he is also a most amazing, caring, and generous human being. He has given me more than I could ever return. It is an honor and privilege to serve Jim, our company, and our clients. Thank you Jim.

Our company continues to grow under the direction of our President, John Hannon. Thank you, John, for steering the ship, and thank you for pushing us all to be better. And, thank you for regularly asking, "When is your book going to be done?" You exemplify the definition of Engaged Management!

And, thank you to Pat Norris. Pat joined our company after a career owning and operating car dealerships. Pat, your real-world insights have been enlightening and I enjoy our impromptu creative sessions—especially from the bow of a fishing boat. I'd like to thank the thousands of local businesses who have allowed me to diagnose your situation and share my advertising recommendations, especially those who embraced my advice, executed it beautifully, and enjoyed the results. It's why I do what I do!

Thank you to the many media outlets that have welcomed me on board, be it for a decade of employment or a couple of weeks of consulting. It's only through these partnerships that I can exercise my marketing chops.

And to my advertising influencers, the colleagues I've learned from over the years, I say thank you. From the spectacular team of Jim Doyle & Associates consultants and our amazing staff at world headquarters in Sarasota, to the many co-workers I've shared a cubicle with and learned lessons from at television, radio, and Internet companies along the way.

A special thank you to Robin Renna for your patience in editing my first book, and to Matt Snelson for your design help.

Finally, and most importantly, I'd like to thank my family, my wife Darlene and our four sons—Benjamin, Connor, Jonathan and Thomas—for allowing me to be away from home so I can do what I love. For all the missed birthdays, Little League games, band concerts and anniversaries, you never complained or made me feel guilty. I'm better on the road because I know life at home is in order... and nothing is better than coming home to you.

Foreword

How would you like to spend the same amount of money on advertising that you do now and get 2-3x more impact? If you did that, how would it affect your bottom line?

You may be about to read the absolute best book on advertising for local businesses that has ever been written. I can say that with some confidence. There are few people in this country who have spent more time reading and studying local advertising than I have. But there's one person who has even more experience than I do. That's Tom Ray.

I have a unique perspective on how smart (and real-world) Tom Ray is. We've worked together for the last 12 years. Almost every week, I hear first-hand about the difference he's made in someone's business. Tom has probably helped more advertisers get the results they deserve than anyone in America. He's helped retailers in hundreds of different categories. He's served medical practices, home services companies, franchises, car dealers, and so many others by sharing the principles that you'll discover in this book.

If you own a business or you're an ad agency or media rep who serves business owners, I encourage you to read this book. Here's why. Whether you spend $3000 per year or $3000 per day on advertising, you (or your clients) deserve to get the absolute maximum possible ROI for that money. In fact, in these crazy, mega-competitive times, you MUST get more impact to deal with a new marketplace and ever-changing competitors.

There's an old line that's usually attributed to a turn-of-the-century retailer in Philadelphia—John Wannamaker. "Half the money I spend on advertising is wasted. I just don't know which half." I find there are so many businesses that can identify with that statement. But that's horrible. Today, you'd better have WAY more than half your advertising performing at a high level. You deserve to, AND accomplishing it will help your business prosper. This book will help you get there quickly. It will help you dramatically increase your ROI.

What I love about this book is that Tom shares some principles that he's seen work over and over. This isn't a theory book. It's loaded with so many actual examples that will make it easy to implement in your business.

Tom Ray has a passion for helping local businesses. He genuinely wants to make a difference. I've seen that up close. He eats, drinks, and sleeps this stuff. He's written a book that can make a difference for you and for your business.

Read it. And hope your competitors don't.

Jim Doyle

INTRODUCTION

Brands are important! Let's make that perfectly clear from the get-go. You should identify your brand, worry about your brand, grow your brand, and protect your brand. As a local business, your brand is defined by the logo you use, the way you answer the phone, and how you greet a customer. Your brand may be defined by an audio identifier (the jingle guys like that term!), a spokesperson, a color scheme. Your brand is affected by the letterhead you choose, the company apparel you wear, your trade show booth, and what community involvement you decide to support. Your brand needs to be carefully planned and maintained with radical consistency. And then, hopefully, over time, the local consumer develops a sense of who you are, what you do and what you stand for, just by being exposed to your brand.

This, however, is a book about advertising. And, while all branding is advertising, all advertising is not branding. For you, the local

1

advertiser, I want to help you not waste precious advertising dollars to simply brand your business. This book is focused on making sure your advertising delivers RESULTS.

It's dangerous to write a book about advertising today. By the time your work hits the virtual bookshelf, the advertising landscape has probably already changed! In fact, it wasn't too long ago that almost every ad said, "Like us on Facebook!" Now, the Facebook "liker" as an advertising currency is old news, and it was less than a year ago (as of this writing) that making your business a Pokemon Go stop was all the rage.

So, it's dangerous to write about advertising because everyone reads with a sense of skepticism, especially in the world of digital advertising where it's a mad dash to find the next "newest," "latest," "hottest" marketing tool or tactic.

That's why this isn't a book focused on the tool or tactic. If you're looking for a read that will guide you through a digital re-targeting strategy that incorporates geo-fencing your competition, you won't find it here. Neither will you find a book that will deliver the Do's and Don'ts of Native Advertising.

So, what is this book?

This is a book based on lessons learned over 30 years of helping the LOCAL advertiser earn better advertising results. And, this book is pretty much media agnostic, meaning it is not meant to be an endorsement of one medium over another. My personal career spans print, radio, broadcast television, cable television and Internet marketing, and, as I have said for years, "They're all good. They can all bring you a new customer."

Instead of predicting the next big digital tool, I'll delve deep into the basic principles of local advertising that need to be in place in order for a campaign to work, regardless of where you decide to invest your advertising money. That said, there will be a healthy dose of digital insights, along with success stories from all different media.

So, who *should* read this book? The answer is simple: anyone who affects an advertising budget. If you're a business owner who handles your own advertising, this book is for you. If you're a marketing director for a business, this book is for you. If you sell advertising and want to be more effective with the campaigns you influence, this book is for you. If you work at an ad agency or in the creative department at a media outlet, this book is for you.

I've broken it down into bite-sized chapters where we'll identify some obvious advertising principles, dispel some longstanding advertising myths, and uncover some new insights. All of the content is designed to help you earn better results from your advertising investment.

Be forewarned. Some of the ideas in this book will fly directly in the face of what most local advertisers believe. Some of the strategies will be contrary to what most local advertisers regularly do. That's okay. Because the content contained in these pages is what we've seen work repeatedly for local advertisers. That means your contradictions are opportunities for improvement. However, you should remember that there are exceptions to everything I'm about to share. So what! I'm much more concerned with what works *consistently* than I am the one-off stories. The "well, one time..." stories don't stack up to a body of work that consistently delivers results.

So, if you're ready, and your mind is open, dig in, discover and deploy...

CHAPTER 1

"I'VE BEEN EVERYWHERE, MAN"

I'm a Johnny Cash fan, and any Johnny fan is familiar with his version of the song, "I've Been Everywhere, Man." Johnny sings, "I've been to Reno, Chicago, Fargo, Minnesota, Buffalo, Toronto, Winslow, Sarasota..." and continues with a rhyming, rambling list of cities he's visited—over 75 different locales by song's end. Every time I hear that song, I think to myself, "That's ME! I've been everywhere, man!"*

For more than a decade, I've traveled this country about 25 weeks a year. Here's a little insight into my life. Every other Sunday I show up at the airport, get on some airline and head off to some destination. Then, on Friday nights I make my way back home. I am certainly a Frequent Flyer! And, when I'm out traveling the country, I have the pleasure of interacting with local advertisers just like you, so I get a chance to see what's working, what's not working and stay ahead of trends, and that's the value proposition I bring to you in this book.

In our company, Jim Doyle & Associates, we have an additional 10 Senior Marketing Consultants who all travel to that same level. I share this with you so that you can feel comfortable that the principles, strategies, and concepts included in this book are all grounded in our feet-on-the-street experience. This is all real-world stuff. I like to say that our research lab is the 90+ cities around the country where we interact with local advertisers every year, and we've been doing this a long time.

In the field, I use this description of Jim Doyle & Associates: "We show LOCAL advertisers, just like you, how to get greater impact from your advertising and marketing. The recurring themes you'll hear are concentration and focus!"

I also want to share this with you. I'm much more "Main Street" than I am "Madison Avenue." By that, I mean our focus is the LOCAL advertiser. If you're Verizon, if you're Apple, if you're Budweiser, I'm not your guy. But if you're a LOCAL advertiser, looking to navigate your way through the ever-changing local advertising landscape, I promise I'll share some powerful concepts and disciplines in the next pages that can dramatically impact the effectiveness of your advertising.

*Of the 78 US cities referenced in Johnny's version of "I've Been Everywhere, Man," I've worked with local advertisers in over half! Sorry, Tallapoosa, I'm sure I'll see you someday.

Chapter 2

"Tradigital"

A s a local advertiser, are you dealing with what many are calling, "The Battle of the Ages" between traditional advertising outlets and the new digital platforms? The struggle of "should I put my advertising money in traditional or digital?" (I see hands raised!)

Let me guess. As a local advertiser, you've got one foot firmly planted in the traditional advertising landscape. What's traditional? We're talking direct mail, newspaper, radio, television... the things on which you probably built your business. And now, over the past few years, you also have a foot over on the digital platform. What's digital? Your SEO, SEM, social, mobile, native advertising, geo-targeting, geo-fencing, and who knows what will be introduced next week! That ground is a little shakier for you; you're just not as familiar with it. And, as an advertiser, you're struggling with that battle, that conflict of, "Where do I invest my resources? Where do I shift

7

my weight?"

What we've come to realize is that it's not a conflict, it's not a battle. We've discovered that the traditional landscape and the digital landscape are actually quite complementary and work well together. The word we use is "tradigital." Our definition of tradigital is the fusion of your traditional advertising with the growing digital landscape. Let's all agree, they're geared for the same end game—to deliver results for your advertising dollar.

The most obvious example of tradigital is using traditional media to drive traffic directly to your website.

The story of "Bob Saves Homes"

Back in the recession, we met with a foreclosure attorney in Michigan. By the way, Michigan was a good place to be a foreclosure attorney during the recession! The auto industry had tanked and there were a lot of hardworking people experiencing some pretty difficult times. In the course of diagnosing his business, we asked a pretty standard question.

"Do you have an online presence Bob?"

"Why of course I do", he answered.

"Well, how would we find you Bob?"

He said, "You'd go to my website."

"Which is?"

He said, "www dot dietrich hyphen law dotnet."

"Three strikes, you're out, Bob."

He said, "Whattya mean!"

We replied, "First off, how do you spell 'Dietrich'? Is it d-i-e, d-e-i...t-r-i-c-h, t-r-i-c-k? You have an easily misspelled last name. That's strike number one. Secondly, you've got a hyphen in your domain! Nobody ever remembers the hyphen. And thirdly, we live in a dotcom world, not dotnet." We said, "Bob, you are what we refer to as 'Domain Name Challenged'."

We continued on with our diagnosis and we asked another of our standard questions. We said, "Bob, in its simplest terms, describe what it is that you do. Break it down to the most basic concept possible and describe what you do."

He pondered it a moment, looked back and said, "I save homes. That's what I do. I save homes. If you're under threat of foreclosure, I can help you stay in your home. I save homes."

Perfect! We came back a few weeks later and said, "Bob, here's your new campaign: Bob saves homes at Bobsaveshomes.com!" We recommended a highly targeted campaign of :15 television commercials that drove traffic directly to his website.

That's "Tradigital." That's using traditional media to drive directly to your digital front door.

We worked with a funeral home and suggested they write a white paper that could be downloaded from their site. We advised getting the domain www.freefuneralguide.com, and then used television to drive traffic to the site for the free download. Tradigital is not a local only concept. In a March, 2016 *Wall Street Journal* article, a Proctor and Gamble representative said, "At P & G, we don't see television and digital as an 'either or,' we see it as an 'and.'"

As a local advertiser, it's important to understand that traditional and digital tools are complementary; they interact and support each other. Don't let the digital world scare you, and don't feel the need to abandon the traditional tools that have worked for you in the past. Lastly, make sure you spend just as much time working on what to say in your message as you do trying to figure out where to say it.

CHAPTER 3

THE MYTH OF THE 3 FREQUENCY

A h, the magic of the 3 frequency. For more than thirty years, I've listened to media sellers, local advertisers, and even ad agencies proclaim the magic of the three frequency. Ever since my earliest days as a radio advertising rep, it's been drilled into my head that "a good schedule has to achieve a 3 frequency!" I clearly recall the rationale:

- **First time, they hear it and think what is it?**
- **Second time, they notice it and think what of it?**
- **Third time, they act on it**

In fact, I did some research and found the origin of the Three Frequency. It can be traced back to 1972, when a Dr. Herbert E. Krugman, then head of market research at GE, published an article in the *Journal of Advertising Research* titled, "Why Three Exposures May Be Enough." In it, Krugman suggests that there are only three levels of exposure:

11

- Curiosity
- Recognition
- Decision

He also suggests there is no such thing as a fourth exposure. Instead, psychologically, exposures four, five, and beyond are simply repeats of the third exposure effect.

And so it was written! In the *Journal of Advertising Research*, by a doctor no less, in 1972. The birth of the Three Frequency!

Today, I cringe every time I hear a media rep tell a client, "…because what you really want to do is achieve a three frequency." I don't buy that three is the desired frequency. I don't buy that something magically happens when a consumer experiences the third exposure to a message.

Firstly, can we agree that any advertising rule created in 1972 is probably outdated? Secondly, understand that Krugman was speaking of the psychological effects of exposures, which don't necessarily correlate to the media effectiveness of exposures. By Krugman's theory, a campaign with a 17 frequency would have no greater effect than a campaign with a 3 frequency. I'm not buying that.

What I can tell you is this—the higher the frequency, the better the campaign will work (when properly targeted, with the right message).

When media salespeople perpetuate the 3 frequency myth, it invites local advertisers to stop buying. For example, if we tell a client that we need to achieve a 3 frequency to make it work, then why, as a client, would I invest in a schedule that delivered a 10 frequency? Shouldn't I stop at three and then take the rest of my budget somewhere else and buy a 3 frequency there?

So, what's the right frequency? After much brain power and internal debate, I think I've come up with the right answer. The right frequency is whatever it takes to get the customer to buy! If it takes 100 times for me to finally order a Sham Wow! then 100 was the right frequency. If it takes 5 times for me to make plans to attend an RV Dealer's open house, then 5 was the right number.

As a local advertiser, ask yourself, "What am I trying to accomplish?" If you're a medical practice that simply wants to announce a new doctor, well that goal will require a lower frequency than the same medical practice trying to fill 25 seats to an educational seminar on their new laser procedure.

Today, when an advertiser asks me, "What's the right frequency?" my answer is typically, "Whatever it takes to get the customer to buy, which means it's probably as much as your budget will allow." Here's what I do know—the more times a message runs, the more chances it has to work. And, the more times a consumer is exposed to a message, the greater the likelihood that they will act.

In 2017, a study by research company YuMe

suggested that a minimum of nine exposures maximizes purchase intent. Results of the study showed that, among overall norms, one video exposure is sufficient to trigger increases across all awareness metrics. However, multiple exposures garner even higher brand awareness scores. On average, for purchase intent and brand favorability, specifically, ads are most effective at a minimum of nine exposures.

I don't know if nine is the right number either, but I do think if we rely on three as the magic number, we are seriously jeopardizing the effectiveness of our precious ad dollars. So, my message is don't focus on a 3 frequency. Focus on delivering as much frequency as you possibly can for the budget allowed, and the higher the frequency, the better.

I'll never forget the marketing guru who once said, "If I've got hemorrhoids, I don't need to see a Preparation H commercial 3 times to go out and buy it!"

And, don't confuse "frequently" with "frequency"! Read on...

CHAPTER 4

"FREQUENTLY DOES NOT EQUAL FREQUENCY"

This is one of the most powerful lessons I've learned in over 30 years of helping local advertisers earn better results. Many businesses confuse "frequently" with "frequency." They think a lot equals effective, that more is better, so 200 commercials must be better than 20 commercials. In local advertising, there's a huge difference between frequently and frequency.

Allow me to demonstrate with this story:

We've already established that I'm a frequent flyer. For more than a decade, I've traveled the country about 25 weeks a year. As I've said, "I've been everywhere, man." For the first five years of doing all this extensive travel, I did it out of the Rochester, NY airport. That's where I lived before I moved to Florida. It was a pretty standard routine. Every other Sunday, I'd show up at the Rochester, NY airport, get on some airline and head off to some destination, and on Friday night

I'd make my way back home.

You know what happens when you become a frequent flyer? You start to recognize people in your home airport, because you're there so much. After a while, you spot the other road warriors and heavy travelers in your market and identify their faces.

Here's what happened to me one Friday night. I'd just arrived at the Rochester airport and it was late. As I was standing at the baggage carousel waiting for my luggage to come down, I casually looked around and spotted a guy who I recognized as someone I saw almost every time I was there.

Well, since I had nothing better to do than stand there waiting for my luggage, I decided to go introduce myself. I said, "I don't mean to bother you, sir, but I see you here all the time... and I know I'm here way too much!"

He said, "You look familiar, too."

Come to find out, his name was Dave, and he was a software trainer who lived in Rochester. Every Monday morning Dave would go to the Rochester, NY airport, get on a Delta Airlines flight, and go to Detroit. His company flew in people from all over the country, and Dave would train them on whatever software they make. On Friday nights, Dave did the reverse, getting on his Delta flight for the return trip from Detroit to Rochester.

Since I fly on Delta a ton, from the very first night that I introduced myself to Dave at the Rochester baggage carousel, I started seeing him on a fairly regular basis—at least once a month, often times a couple of times a month. We were even able to sit together on many flights, and we developed a bit of a friendship.

For the next couple of years, I saw Dave regularly, once or twice a month. Then, for reasons unknown, one month goes by, two months go by, three, maybe four months go by, and I've seen hide nor hair of my new buddy, Dave. Oh well...

Then, one Friday night, I'm in the Detroit airport making my way home. As I approach the Rochester, NY gate, lo and behold, who's standing there? Dave. I walked right up to him and said, "Dave, buddy, how ya doin'!"

He said, "Tom, I haven't seen you for a while, have you been traveling as much?"

I said, "Oh my gosh, I've been everywhere, man!"

And, as frequent flyers do, Dave looks at me and whispers, "Did you get your first class upgrade?"

I smiled, and with a thumbs up, said, "Yes I did!"

The announcement is made, "First class may now board," and Dave and I go walking onto the plane. We sit side by side, and here's where the magic occurs.

Down the aisle comes the flight attendant. She's carrying a tray and on the tray is one can of James Page Ale. She walks right up to Dave and says, "Hey Dave! You're in luck! We have James Page tonight!" She sets the can of beer in front of him, steps back and says, "No glass, right?"

Dave replies, "That's right Linda."

She looks and me and says, "Can I get you a pre-flight beverage, sir?"

I said, "I'll have a Bud."

She replied, "Be right back!" and turned and walked away.

I looked at Dave and said, "What just happened here?"

He said, "Whattya mean?"

I said, "What do I mean?! She knows your name, she knows what you drink, she knows you don't take a glass. How does that happen?"

He said, "Tom, that's Linda. Her crew works this flight all the time. I'm on this flight every Friday night." He continued, "You travel more miles in a year than I do, you must have a connection like that with some flight crew, somewhere..."

I said, "Dave, I got nuthin'!"

And then it struck me.

I fly frequently.

Dave flies with frequency.

In advertising terms, Dave is on the same

channel, on the same programs, on the same days on the same weeks, every single month. Everyone in his market knows his name, they know what he drinks, and they know he doesn't take a glass.

I spend more money on advertising than Dave does. But I'm on different channels, on different programs, at different times, on different days, on different weeks... and nobody in my market has a clue who I am.

If you're responsible for an advertising budget, you must understand: FrequentLY does NOT equal FrequenCY. What you're after is FrequenCY!

CHAPTER 5

"TO DO LIST" ADVERTISING

D o you keep a "To Do" list? Do you keep a short list of things that have to get done sometime in the immediate future? Maybe you just keep a mental list of "gotta get that done" items like scheduling an oil change for the car, or making that dental appointment or calling for that bathroom remodel estimate. Today, a "to do" list can be mental, it might be on your smart phone, or it might even be kept by "Alexa" on your Amazon Echo!

My wife is a Master To Do List-er! She keeps a little notepad on our kitchen counter that has all the things she needs to get done to keep our household running smoothly. Do you know when she spends the most time updating and checking her To Do list? It's Sunday evening as she readies herself for the week. Like most folks, my wife starts each week with a set of goals she wants to accomplish for the week. Which is why I'm such a

21

fan of what I call, "To Do List Advertising."

"To Do List Advertising" is simply the concept of running aggressive vertical campaigns early in the week to get the advertiser on the consumer's To Do List. I like this tactic for three reasons...

1) Immediacy
2) High Frequency
3) Less Clutter

Immediacy. I love the idea of aggressively running Saturday, Sunday, and early Monday to drive Monday phone calls. Most people attack their To Do List on Monday, so running vertically over the weekend and early Monday morning puts the advertiser closest to the desired action.

High Frequency. Running concentrated campaigns over a couple of days results in higher frequency. I'd much rather have an advertiser run 15 commercials in two days than run 20 over the course of a week or month!

Less Clutter. Typically, early week advertising avoids the classic retail clutter of late week. Leave Wednesday, Thursday, and Friday to the car dealers and furniture stores that still believe they have to drive weekend traffic.

Who's a good candidate for To Do List advertising? Kitchen remodelers, replacement windows, roofing and siding guys, home services that are more want than need (as opposed to plumbers and HVAC businesses). Law services like Social Security Disability and Bankruptcy are good candidates. Health services that aren't emergencies, such as dentists, podiatrists, and lab procedures are good candidates. Insurance is a To Do list category.

We've even seen a very successful Saturday/Sunday/early Monday campaign from a Personal Injury attorney who knows that many accidents occur over the weekend. The message is, "If you've been hurt over the weekend, call us. We're here for you 24/7."

Peter Drucker said, "Concentration is the key to all economic success!" and early week concentration to affect the consumer's To Do list is a smart technique.

CHAPTER 6

DON'T CHASE THE EXTREMES

One of the few critical elements to all successful local advertising campaigns is to "Target the Right Audience." (I know what you're thinking. I paid for a book to tell me to target the right audience? Duh!) Of course. Nobody is going to argue that. No one is going to insist that they've "targeted the wrong audience for years, it works beautifully every time!" While I'm sure you understand targeting the right audience, there's a critical adjunct to the rule...

Target the right audience AND don't chase the extremes! Chasing the extremes is an all-too-common local advertising mistake.

Let me explain. If you can clearly define your core (and I hope as soon as you hear the word "core" you immediately have a specific mental image of exactly WHO drives your business), that's where you want to put all of your efforts and energies. Place your core in the center of the target—the bullseye—because they carry the highest value. Outside of the target, you have what we call "extremes." What's an extreme? By definition, extremes are those who engage your business who don't fit your nice, tight core description.

I know that every once in a while someone stumbles into your showroom, calls your office or visits your website who doesn't fit your nice, tight core description. I get it, it happens. The mistake we make as advertisers, however, is we tend to focus on those extremes because they stand out. So when that someone stumbles into our showroom, we notice. We step back and say, "Wow, we don't typically see that profile here..." The mistake we make is when we think, "Hmmm, maybe there are more just like that person that I'm missing. If I just took a little bit of my budget and went after that audience, we could see a spike!"

That's when I grab you and focus you right back on your core. My saying when I encounter this is, "Take all the wood, put it behind the tip of the arrow, and go right after who drives your business!"

I know what you're thinking. "Of course Tom, I get this, move on..."

I have to tell you, **I see this mistake all the time.** All the time!

Let me share one of my favorite road warrior stories with you. It happened in Fargo, North Dakota. Fargo's not a very big town. I had just landed and had a quick 8-minute cab ride from the airport to my hotel. On the ride, I suddenly yell to the driver, "Stop!" so I can get out and take a picture of this billboard:

Now, what do you think the answer from Mrs. Rejuv, of rejūv Skin & Laser Clinic, would be if we asked her, "What percent of your laser hair removal clientele is male?" Would it be, "Less than 5%"?

"Then what are you trying to do with this billboard, double it to less than 10%?!"

Trust me, if he's in Fargo, and he needs manscaping, he will seek you out!

Focus on the core, don't chase the extremes!

A couple of years ago, Harley Davidson informed all their dealers that the fastest growing new Harley owner group was women! And, inevitably, every Harley dealer I met with around the country began

27

to ask me to help them target women. So I would ask them, "If you sold 50 new motorcycles next month, how many would be purchased by women?" You know what kind of answers I got? "Two, maybe three." And I'd say, "so why would you take your foot off the gas of what you know drives your business (middle aged men) to chase what might amount to maybe 10% of your business?"

A Classic "Chasing the Extremes" Story

A few years ago I met with a casino in the Southwest. I sat for an hour with the marketing director and peppered him with questions to help me understand who they were and what separated them from every other casino in the area. In the conversation, I learned:

- **This casino has over 1,000 slot machines on the gaming floor**
- **That's more slot machines than any other casino in the area**
- **Women over the age of 50 are the typical slot player**
- **The slot machines are responsible for over 60% of this casino's revenues**

What do you think this casino marketing director answered when I asked, "Who do you try to target with your advertising?"

He said, "Well, Tom, we'd really like to see more young couples coming in. If we can get them to come in to celebrate a birthday or anniversary, feed them dinner, then get them down on the gaming floor, that's really who we target with our advertising."

Let me get this straight. You have over 1,000 slot machines on the floor. That's more slots than any other casino in the area. Slots are what drive your revenues. Women 50+ play slots. But you'd like to target younger couples? Don't chase those extremes!

I've been in casinos all across the country and I can tell you who the core is. It's that lovely, senior woman sitting at the slot machine. Any time, day or night, she's there.

Focus on your core, don't chase the extremes. The more clearly defined your core, the more effective your advertising. And with today's digital offerings, you can zero in on your core with pinpoint accuracy. It wasn't that long ago that ad campaigns were based simply on an age range and gender. Today's campaigns are based on keyword searches, website interactions, purchase history, mobile geography, and more. It's almost like you barely think of a product or service, and before you know it, you're seeing ads for that very category pop up in your Facebook feed!

CHAPTER 7

I HATE ADULTS, 25-54

I've had the pleasure of meeting with thousands of local advertisers over the years. I ask every one of them, "Who do you try to target with your advertising?" Sometimes I'll get an answer like this, "Well, Tom, our demo is 'Adults, 25 to 54.'"

Adults, 25 to 54? Come on. You would never describe your customer, your client, your prospect, your patient, "Adults 25 to 54," if it weren't for media people giving you that language.

By the way, Adults 25 to 54 isn't a target... that's a family reunion! There's nothing that a 25-year-old male has in common with a 50-year-old female.

Frankly, while A25-54 has become a kind of catch-all for many advertisers, I think it's still way too broad in most cases. Everything I know about advertising says to focus.

Here are the kinds of questions I ask that help uncover a clearer picture of a client's core. I'll start with the physical characteristics...

1) If I sat here all day with you and watched your traffic, who would I see come through the doors?
2) Who would walk through to make you say, "That's the perfect 'up'"?
3) Geographically, where do your customers come from? Can you say that 50% of your customers come from what mile radius?
4) Are they working? Do they have kids? What kind of jobs do they have?
5) What is their income? What is the average value of their home?

Then, I'll move to more emotional characteristics...

1) What pain are your core customers in to make them come to see you?
2) What are they looking for out of life?
3) What are they not getting?
4) What problem are they attempting to solve when they buy your product or service?

I'll also ask advertisers to describe what their "ideal" prospect looks like. Sometimes, the ideal customer can be a different description than what the actual core is, so I like to understand the nuances.

One thing I want to make sure you understand: if you're working with a limited budget, it's best to start with the narrowest target possible. *A broad target and a small budget = disaster.* Frankly, many local advertisers don't have a big enough budget to try and reach "Adults, 25 to 54!"

By the way, you should WANT to have a better target! By having a well-defined target, you can:

- **Save money.** By not wasting it trying to reach people who aren't hungry for your offer
- **Save time.** By not wasting it on unqualified prospects who may respond
- **Sell easier.** Because you know exactly who your customer is and what they want
- **Create a clearer message.** It's easier to write an effective message for the ideal prospect than it is to write for a broad audience
- **Command a higher price.** By knowing exactly who your product fits and what they'll pay for it

Finally, it's okay that your media outlet of choice reaches a huge audience. That's fine, because tucked in that huge audience is your target. You just need to strategically sift through that audience and find the VERY BEST places (just a few, though) to reach the bullseye, and it ain't Adults 25 to 54!

CHAPTER 8

DETERMINING YOUR CORE

How does an advertiser determine their core? I like to start very simply with age and gender, and I like to focus on a nice tight twenty-year age range. I love when I meet with a local advertiser who says, "We try to target people in their 40's and 50's." Perfect! We're going to target from 40 to 60! Think narrow with your age range and force yourself to get zeroed in on exactly who drives your business.

Next, we determine gender—male or female—which will be determined by your category. I must tell you, after 30+ years in local advertising, which includes thousands and thousands of local advertiser interactions across every category imaginable, I'm convinced that women drive 80% of all purchase decisions in this country! I'm firmly convinced of it. You'd be hard-pressed to find too many categories where she doesn't drive the purchasing decisions.

Here's another road warrior story for you.

I was in a Mid-Atlantic market, meeting with the local ReBath franchise. You're probably familiar with ReBath, the over-the-tub, "get a new bathroom in a day" product. We were having a productive dialogue about his business and then it came time for me to ask, "So, who do you try to target with your advertising?"

He looked at me very matter-of-factly and said, "Tom, here's my customer... a homeowner, somewhere between 45 and 65 years of age. They've been in the home ten-plus years. The home is valued somewhere between $100K and $250K. And frankly, Tom, most of my customers live in one of these five zip codes."

Spot on! I loved that answer! Nice and narrow.

I said, "Terrific! Hey, let me ask you... male or female?"

He looked at me and said, "Tom, in my category it's both, really. Both."

I paused for a few seconds, and then said, "Can I challenge you on that?"

He took offense. In fact, he started tapping the table and said, "Tom, I'm telling you, it's both." He looked me in the eye and insisted, "We won't even schedule the in-home visit unless they can guarantee that both husband and wife will be there! I'm telling you, it's both."

I said, "I get that, and I understand why you won't go into the home unless they're both there.

But, let me ask you this, who called to schedule the in-home visit?"

We both knew the answer. She did.

In fact, the line I used was this, "A husband and a wife wake up one morning, one of them turns to the other and says, 'Honey, I really think it's time for a bathroom remodel.' Who just said that?"

Not "...it's time for a bass boat," but "it's time for a bathroom remodel." She did!

So ask yourself—in your category, who wants this to happen? Who's driving the decision? Who's going to go online and do the research? Who's going to pick up the phone and make the calls? Frankly, who's going to drag me out on a Saturday morning and say, "Today is the day we are buying a new mattress!" In almost all categories, you'll find that it's her, it's her, it's her!

The next thing I want to explore when determining your core, is what I call "triggers." My "triggers" question goes like this:

"What just happened in your best prospect's world that made them finally engage your business?"

In other words, what are the triggers that prompted someone to walk into your showroom or call your office or visit your website?

I want you to understand how critical it is to identify your category's triggers. Why do most of you reading this book spend money on advertising? If I collected all of your answers, you know what it would boil down to? "To get a new customer. To see a new face." That's the Holy Grail for most local advertisers, unless yours is a high recurring sales cycle category. Even then, if I could convince you that I had a sure-fire strategy to drive a steady stream of newbies—the right newbies—you'd listen!

So the question is: what are the triggers that drive the first interaction with your prospect?

Triggers can be obvious. If you're a plumber, what's the trigger? A clogged drain. A roofer? A leaky roof. A chiropractor? "I crawled to the bathroom this morning!"

Sometimes triggers aren't so obvious.

A few years ago, I was meeting with a senior living center in a market. There were three people from the senior living center and myself involved in the conversation. We had just finished talking about the target in senior living and they convinced me, quite easily, that the target in senior living is NOT the 83-year-old. It's the adult children of the senior, specifically, it's the oldest daughter. It almost always rests on her shoulders to do the research, gather the siblings, and make the tough call. I'm totally on board with that. I get it.

So, I asked my triggers question, "What just happened in the adult children's worlds that made them finally come in for their first tour? What was the trigger that made them come in and kick your tires?"

Here's what I heard:

"Slip and fall." Mom had a slip and fall, a burn, some sort of household accident. Here come the kids.

"Doctor referral." The doctor called the kids and said, "Your Dad isn't taking his medications correctly, he cannot be home by himself anymore." Here come the kids.

"Death of a spouse." Here come the kids.

One of the representatives from the senior living center looked at me and said, "Oh! The Holidays! The Holidays are a very real trigger in our category."

She saw my confused look and continued, "Oh yeah. The Holidays are often the first time in a few months—six months, even ten months—that all the kids are together. They all gather at Mom's to celebrate the holidays, and at the end of the evening, they start talking. One says, 'Have you noticed Mom's lost weight?' And another says, 'Yeah, and the house is a mess. She always kept a beautiful house.' Finally, another sibling will join the conversation and say, 'Hey guys. I just found the iron... in the FREEZER! Guys, we gotta do something.'"

Turns out the holidays are a very real trigger in senior living.

So, we ran that campaign. January 1st, a few years ago, in Knoxville, TN. We put a 55-year-old on television who said, "I came home for the holidays. I noticed Mom had lost weight, the house was a mess. I knew it was time to call Brookview."

The result? Brookview's phone exploded with calls. We clearly identified the triggers in the category.

Finally, the third thing I want to explore when defining the core after age/gender and triggers is what I call my "Questions question." My "Questions question" goes like this:

What are the three or four common questions every newbie asks when they engage your business for the first time?

In other words, if you and I stood shoulder-to-shoulder and watched your door pulls, or we stood over your phone and waited for the next newbie to call in, when that phone rang, what would you elbow me and say, "I can already tell you what they're going to ask..."?

You know what your new prospects will ask, you hear the same questions day in and day out.

There are a couple of questions that are fairly universal across all categories and you can already guess what they are. The first is "how much?" Every newbie wants to know how much something costs first. The second is "how long?" or some element of time—how long does delivery take? How soon can you get here? How much down time will I experience?

And then questions three and four will depend on the category. For example, if you're in healthcare, what does everyone ask on the very first call? "Is this covered by my insurance?" If nine out of ten prospects ask the insurance question, that's critical information!

Determine your core, discover their triggers, determine their questions, think narrow, and all of this goes far beyond, "My demo is adults 25 to 54."

CHAPTER 9

WWSD

Here's an exercise to help you better focus on your core. It's called WWSD, "What Would Sally Do?"

As we move beyond media generated parameters, like Adults 25 to 54, and look to more accurately describe who our target is, this exercise involves your entire organization and can be eye-opening.

The idea is to break your organization down into your separate departments and have each one create a personality profile of who they think is your average customer. Then, bring the different profiles together and hammer it out until you've come up with an individual profile, that the whole company can agree on, of exactly who drives your business. The goal is that now every advertising question moving forward must answer, "What would this particular individual, who best represents our target, do?" In other words, what would Sally do, if "Sally" is who we all agree is our

43

specific target.

Make sure you break your organization down into the various departments, as each will have a unique perspective on who they believe is the target. Have your sales department create a profile, your in-the-field techs or front-liners create a profile, your back office support create a profile, even the C-suite creates their own profile of what your target looks like. Allow each department to get together, give them a time limit, a half hour should do the trick, supply them a white board and markers and let the exercise take shape.

The key to this exercise is to be as specific as possible and assign an identity to this profile as an end result. So, your target no longer is working women between the ages of 25 and 49, it's Sally, mother of 3, married to Bill. She's 41 years old and works as a nurse. Bill, 43, works at the plant. Sally drives a leased crossover, Bill drives an SUV. They have three children—Billy and Benjamin play baseball, Ashley is into cheerleading. At the conclusion of the exercise, you know where they live, what the household income is, you've identified what motivates their buying decisions, and more.

I first did this exercise when I was on the sales staff of a Classic Rock radio station. We broke our entire radio station staff into our respective departments. The sales staff went into one room, the on-air personalities in another, our promo team in another, and our internal support staff in another. After a half hour, we all came together to present our target individual. About the only thing we all agreed on at the start was gender. As a classic rocker, each department agreed our target was male. We were all pretty close on age, but when it came to other identifiers, each department saw things differently. The sales team created an upscale, import-driving professional, while our promo department and on-air talent identified a hard-working, blue-collar, truck-driving target. As one talent said, "Have you ever seen who comes to our remotes?"

Another time, I was training this concept with a television sales staff in Wisconsin. At the end of the session, the station news director who had been in the training approached me and said, "Debbie Durowski!"

"Excuse me?" I replied.

"Debbie Durowski," he repeated proudly. "That's our Sally."

He proceeded to tell me that he had done this exercise with his news department. They identified Debbie Durowski as their typical viewer, and everyone in the news department knew her name, they knew where she lived, they knew everything about her. They knew her two biggest concerns were the safety of her children and the health of her aging parents. They knew her dream was to take the kids to Disney just once while they were still young.

In fact, he showed me the giant white easel sheet with her profile on it that he had prominently displayed in their newsroom. He said, "Tom, whenever I see a reporter struggling with a story, I march them in front of the profile and say, 'Write it so it matters to Debbie.'"

Here's the workbook page from my advertising workshop I often do with a small group of local advertisers:

-The "Sally" Exercise-

With as much detail as possible, describe your IDEAL prospect Profile. Give this person an identity.

- Age: _____
- Gender: _____
- Relationship status: _____
  (married, single, divorced...)
- Occupation: _____
- HHI: $_____
- Family: _____
- Goals, dreams, desires, wishes: _____
  _____
  _____
- How do they like to be sold? _____
  _____
  _____
- What pain are they in? _____
  _____
- Name: _____

Imagine getting your company to a point where absolutely everyone is on board and every employee from every department has a crystal clear picture of who your target is. Imagine how much easier advertising decisions would be once you only have to answer to a single individual who represents your entire target.

"Gee, should we buy a billboard in the minor league ball park for $12,000 for the season?" Well, what would Sally do (or Debbie or whomever is your profile)?

Well, Sally has two sons and they both play Little League baseball and the only time Sally ever gets to the minor league park is when the team hosts Little League night and the boys get to go to the game in their uniforms and run the bases after the game. So, does that seem worth the $12,000 investment? Probably not.

What about spending $1,500 to sponsor the Breast Cancer Awareness Walk? Well, Sally is a nurse. She had an aunt who battled breast cancer so she's sensitive to the issue, and there are going to be a lot of people who are just like Sally at the walk. So maybe that's an investment worth making.

Not only does the WWSD exercise make it easier for you to choose where to invest your advertising dollars, it also makes the creative process more effective. It's much easier to write an ad for Sally than it is to write an ad for "Women, 25 to 54." Once you have a specific individual in your head, it's way easier to tell that person a story and create a response than try to persuade a nameless, faceless demographic.

"Write it so it matters to Debbie!"

CHAPTER 10

THE MESSAGE

Once you've determined your core and you've decided whom to talk to, the question then becomes, "What do we tell them? What's the right message?"

Here's how I've described it for local advertisers: your message must convey your distinction, be consistent across everything you do, and be singular.

There's a lot packed into that one sentence, so let's break it down. Let's start with that word "distinction." Different marketers refer to this in different ways, but what we're basically after here is, "what is your differentiator"? What can you, as a business, firmly plant your flag in and say, "Here's who we are," with respect to the competitive landscape. You want to plant your flag in something that the other guys either cannot lay claim to, or haven't yet, so you can be the first to do so. We know in marketing that it's better to be first than to be better! There are a lot of better mouse traps out there, but, "First in always wins!"

What's your distinction, your differentiator—that one very specific reason why a prospect should choose you over anyone else in your category? Professional marketers refer to this as your USP, your Unique Selling Proposition. Simply, what makes you stand out from the rest of your competition.

Here's an analogy. The mind of the consumer works like a file cabinet. For any given category, there's a file in the brain of the consumer. The consumer is exposed to a category, their big file cabinet brain pops up, a drawer opens, and up pops a file for that category. The advertiser's goal is to be the first name that pops out the top of that file. That's easy, we can all understand that.

Now, let's complicate it a little bit. The more cluttered the category—the thicker the file—the harder it's going to be and the more it's going to cost to be the first name that pops up. If you're in a highly cluttered, highly competitive category—a thick file—it's going to be harder and will cost you more to be the first name that pops up in the mind of the consumer.

So, the question is if you're in a highly competitive category—a cluttered, thick file—what's the very best thing you can do as an advertiser?

The answer is to get out of that file and create

a whole new file!

If you're in a cluttered, competitive, noisy category and everyone is jockeying for position and spending money, let them duke it out. Get out of that file and create your own.

The classic example I use in my presentations is the shampoo file. Picture any shampoo aisle in any grocery store or drug store in Anytown, USA. Talk about cluttered! It's shelf space after shelf space of bottles, tubes and dispensers, covered by every label and logo imaginable. That's a competitive category, a very cluttered file.

If, however, I said to you, "dandruff shampoo," you immediately see a bottle of Head and Shoulders in your mind's eye. Procter & Gamble, the makers of Head and Shoulders, gets it. They knew they couldn't be number one in the highly cluttered, highly competitive shampoo file, so they got out of it and created their own file, "The dandruff shampoo" file, and they own it!

Your job, as a local advertiser, is to determine, or better yet, create, a file in the mind of the consumer that you, and only you, can own.

Let me give you some examples.

If you can't be your market's "divorce attorney," maybe you could be the "divorce attorney for men."

If the dental category is cluttered, maybe you could claim the market's "sedation dentist" position.

If you can't be the market's biggest Ford dealer, maybe you could be the "Ford Truck Headquarters." If the Ford Truck position is already taken, maybe you could get even narrower and be the F150 Outlet.

Create a whole new file.

If you are not the oldest, biggest, most dominant, instantly thought of, category-leading player in your market, you need to create a file in the mind of the consumer that you can own.

"Funeral homes" is a highly competitive category in any market, and in every market, there are typically one or two—maybe even three—long-standing players that make everybody's short list. So, if you're a funeral home in that type of competitive environment and you are NOT on that short list, the best thing you can do is create a whole new file. Get out of the funeral home file and create a new file.

"The discount funeral home"? Don't laugh, it's an awesome position to own! We've worked with many funeral homes who told us, "We don't charge as much as the big guys, but we don't know how to say that properly in an ad campaign." We've helped many of them claim the "less expensive funeral" position and experience dramatic results.

"The cremation experts." The CANA (Cremation Association of North America) announced that in 2015 cremation surpassed traditional burial for the first time ever in the US. The cremation rate was almost 49%, nationwide, compared to the National Funeral Directors Association burial rate estimate of 45%.

"The Military Funeral Experts." We worked with a funeral home that was struggling with their advertising campaign. Once we discovered they were very good at military burials and that the funeral director was a former Marine, we helped them claim that position. They reported an immediate increase in click-throughs on their digital campaign once they changed the creative to claim the military positon, and they also reported an increase in services, especially from a larger geographical area.

If I say, "funeral homes in your city," you can probably come up with a few names. But if I say, "affordable funeral home" or "cremation expert" or "military funeral specialists," can you think of one name? If not, those are files waiting to be claimed. Whoever claims them first becomes number one in that file.

Determine, or better yet, create a file in the mind of the consumer that you and only you can own, or as I like to say, "Find a niche and scratch it!"

Find that one thing that you do that nobody else in your category does, or has claimed yet, and scratch it! Meaning, once you find that thing you do differently, that's what you focus on in your message; that's what you shout from the rooftops, because everything else is equal.

I see way too many local advertisers wasting valuable creative time and space touting things that any of their competitors could just as easily claim. If the other guys can say it too, then skip it and find something else to be the focus of your message.

Find a niche and scratch it!

CHAPTER 11

FIND YOUR "ONE THING"

It's a classic scene from the classic movie, *City Slickers*. Crusty old cowboy, Curley, shares with Mitch, a man in a midlife crisis, the secret of life: "One thing. Just one thing... and that's what you've got to figure out."

To be honest, the first time I saw that scene, I didn't get it.

I remember going to see *City Slickers* when it came out in 1991, and I remember vividly when the famous "one thing" scene came on the screen. Here I was, sitting in the theater, enjoying the heck out of the movie with Curley and Mitch out on the range. Curley turns to Mitch and asks, "You know what the secret to life is?" I leaned forward in my theater seat thinking, *this should be good...*

Mitch replies, "No. What?"

Curley, holding up his index finger, says, "This."

Mitch wisecracks, "Your finger?"

Curley responds, "One thing, just one thing.

55

You stick to that and everything else don't mean shit."

Mitch asks the obvious question, the one I was thinking, "That's great, so what's the one thing?"

Curley points to Mitch and growls, "That's what you've got to figure out..."

At that moment, I was completely confounded. The lesson was totally lost on me. I didn't get it. I remember walking out of the movie that night thinking to myself, *that was a great movie, but I totally didn't get the one thing scene!*

Twenty years later, I was sitting on my couch one weekend, flipping through the channels, and I came upon *City Slickers*. Remembering how much I loved it, I started watching. The "one thing" scene came on and it hit me like a ton of bricks! *Holy cow! Now I get it! That's what I do!*

Twenty-five times a week, twenty-five weeks a year, I meet with local advertisers. My goal is to help each of you find the key to your business life. You want to know what it is? It's "one thing, just one thing." You stick to that, and nothing else matters!

Your goal, as an advertiser, as a business, is to determine what your one thing is. What do you do that separates you as better than all of your competition? What can you claim that makes you the best choice in your category?

Here's your next exercise. As soon as you can,

carve out a half hour of private time—a time and place when you can really focus—and answer this question for your business: Our one thing is _____.

Try to be as specific as possible. Think about your business, your company and what separates you from your competition. For some of you reading this, the answer is obvious. Your company has some distinct advantage that makes you the better choice. For most reading this, the answer isn't so obvious. You'll struggle trying to pinpoint your "one thing."

Answering these types of questions should help you:

- What do we do that no one else in our category does?
- What can we claim that no one else can claim (or hasn't yet)?
- What special skill do we possess?
- What piece of equipment do we have that no one else in our competitive landscape has?
- What line do we carry exclusively in our market?
- What's our singular focus?
- What's our special offer?
- What major designation have we achieved that none of our competitors have?

Simply put, why should someone come see you

vs. anyone else in your competitive landscape?

Here's another suggestion. Once you think you've clearly uncovered your one thing, go ask five other people in your organization to tackle this exercise. Pick five others in your company, from the highest office down to your front-liners, and have them answer, "What's our one thing?" Give them a quiet place and a half hour and have them answer, as specifically as possible the question, "Why should someone choose us over everyone else in our competitive landscape?" Or, you may want to gather your five-member panel in a room at the same time, show them the *City Slickers* clip (simply YouTube "*City Slickers* one thing"), and have them privately write down what they think your company's one thing is. Then, collect the answers and have a good discussion, the goal of which is to commonly define what your company's one thing is.

Now, here's where it gets interesting. If you ask five people in your organization, "What's our one thing?" and you get five different answers, well, there's your first red flag! If you don't know internally why someone should choose you over the competition, how do you expect your customer externally to know?

Your "one thing" should be specific, measurable, demonstrative, and true. Then the goal of your advertising message is to make that obvious.

CHAPTER 12

"IT'S OUR CUSTOMER SERVICE THAT MAKES THE DIFFERENCE!"

After doing the exercise in our last chapter on finding your "one thing," I wonder how many of you have started down this path: "Well, it's really our customer service that makes the difference. We put such an emphasis on better customer service. In fact, we hear horror stories from our customers on how they were treated by our competition. So, really, the number one reason to choose us over anyone else is the better buying experience we offer. It's our customer service that makes the difference…"

If you've started down that path as your "one thing," here's what I would recommend—put it in reverse, back up, and go find something else because it won't work.

From an advertising perspective, CUSTOMER SERVICE IS NOT A DIFFERENTIATOR!

The reason is pretty obvious. It's because you and I, as consumers, ain't buyin' it.

Everyone makes the claim of better customer service, and isn't it amazing that American consumers think that customer service in this country stinks! So, businesses can claim it, but no one believes it. Nobody reading this right now will ever be motivated to jump off the sofa and make a purchase decision because someone promises "a better buying experience."

Yet, we hear it all the time in local advertising, across every category imaginable. In fact, it's the most common answer to our question, "So why should I come shop you versus anyone else in your competitive landscape?"

"Well ya know Tom, it really is our customer service…"

Or,

"We treat ya better!"

"It's our people who make the difference"

"For a better buying experience…"

This is all cliché blah, blah in the minds of the consumer.

I love the time I met with a business owner who spent a half hour describing how customer service was the big differentiator between his business and the competition. He took great pride in telling me about his staff expertise and how well they took care of customers. At the height of his customer service chest-thumping, the phone rang. Since there were no other employees in the building I asked if he needed to answer it. His response: "Nah, I'll let the machine get it..." Are you kidding me?!

The bottom line? I've yet to find the local advertising campaign that launched a business to the stratosphere by saying, "We treat you better." As my mentor, Jim Doyle, says, "Customer service isn't something you claim. That's something you earn." You earn it AFTER they've already engaged your business, which means you have to find something else that will bring them to your front door.

Now, don't get me wrong. Excellent customer service is critical to the success of any local business, no doubt. I suggest you establish ultra-high standards of customer service from all of your employees, especially those who connect directly with your prospects and customers. I am not downplaying the importance of excellent customer service. The mistake that many advertisers make, however, is that they want to focus on customer service as the main reason to choose them over the competition, and that falls on deaf ears, because we've all had way too many bad customer service personal experiences.

Even service industries struggle with good customer service. Trust me, as a road warrior I could bore you to tears with service industry let-downs. I experience them every week. Like the front desk rep at a major hotel chain who responded to my simple request to bill my two-night stay separately so I could do expenses more easily. "Uh, yeah. I can't do that." Or the rental car company that couldn't add a second driver to the reservation over the phone. Or the major airline that... well, let's not even go there.

So, why do so many local businesses land on customer service as their one thing? It's usually because they haven't spent any time trying to really discover a true differentiator. Call it lazy, call it stubborn, call it unaware, call it naiveté, call it whatever you want. I find that most businesses don't dig deep enough to establish their differentiator because they think claiming customer service will work.

"Gee Tom, if everyone believes customer service is awful, shouldn't I tout the better experience I offer as a way to win a customer and beat the competition?" I wish it worked that way, but it just doesn't. The public has been burned too many times. I've met with tons of advertiser who insist they really do deliver a better buying experience, and that should be the focus of their message. I used to argue. I used to try to point out that it won't work. Now, when someone answers the "why you instead of your competition" question with some version of "better customer service," I simply say, "Great, and what else?"

When everybody touts something that nobody

believes, it's advertising waste.

Two advertising pet peeves of mine:

1) "It's our people who make the difference"
2) "I am, I am, I am __(insert business name)__"

I was watching a local newscast and heard an announcer say, "...sponsored by Northwest Bank, where it's our people that make the difference!" Really? Is that the best you can do? I can just hear the ad agency asking the bank president, "Now why should someone switch to your bank?" and the bank president responding, "Well, really, it's our people that make the difference." Well then. If you say so!

"Our people make the difference" is, as my colleague Don Fitzgibbons, the Guru of Ads, would say, "Complete blah, blah. It says nothing, means nothing, and will result in nothing!"

Now, what if that bank focused on a real benefit, like extended hours. (I know, everyone does banking online, but think of the small business owners who have daily deposits.) Would a specific benefit as simple as extended hours do more to put that bank on the banking map, to create a file in the mind of the consumer? I'd say so.

There's a bank in the South that is open 7am-7pm on weekdays. It's something they hang their hat on. In fact, their front door handles are shaped as the number seven! "Open 7am to 7pm" is a very specific and distinct differentiator. It may not matter to all, but it will definitely matter to some, like the small business owner!

So I ask you, which is more effective:

"Northwest Bank, it's our people that make the difference!"

Or

"Liberty Bank, open every weekday, 7am to 7pm!"

At least the Liberty Bank slogan offers something tangible. And, from a guy who has personally met with dozens and dozens of marketing directors at banks and credit unions all over the country, I'm hard-pressed to recall the marketing position of any, except I do remember Liberty Bank, open 7am to 7pm.

Also, what's with the "I am, I am, I am" creative craze? You've seen this creative concept. Fast-cut edits of different people proclaiming, "I am" and the last face finishes it for all, "I am (insert business name)." I suppose it's a business's cool way of saying "It's our people!" Again, I can just hear the ad agency creative pow-wow, "Their big differentiator is their people. So, let's highlight a bunch of different, good-looking employee faces all saying 'I am'. We'll get a nice, diverse cross section of faces from all their different departments, we'll edit them together, and the last one will say the business name!" Big institutions like hospitals, utilities, and banks love to use this technique. I watch those ads and I think, "Great. And I am Tom Ray. So what."

I now live in Florida and there's a company (or business or something) down here called Mosaic. They do something with agriculture. The first few years I lived here, I'd regularly see their TV commercials and they used the "I am, I am, I am... Mosaic" concept. After seeing their ads for about two years, my wife turned to me one morning and said, "So what do they do?" My reply, "Damned if I know!" I've lived in Florida almost a decade and I still really have no idea what they do, why I should care and what they want me to do as a result of their advertising, and they spend a ton on advertising!

CHAPTER 13

"THE SIXTY DAY WALK ON IT WARRANTY"

Let me introduce you to a friend of mine, Michelle Laws. She and her husband own Law's Abbey Flooring Center. I first met Michelle in August of 2009 in Jonesboro, Arkansas, when I had the pleasure of taking her through the Jim Doyle & Associates client diagnosis process—a series of targeted questions designed to uncover important information about a business that will lead to an advertising strategy. Michelle and I had been talking about her target, what drives her business, trends, seasonality, and the such. Next, I wanted to find out about the competitive landscape in the flooring category there in Jonesboro, AR in the summer of '09.

I asked, "Michelle, if my wife and I were homeowners here in Jonesboro, and we decided it was time for... wait, and SHE decided it was time for new flooring (see Chapter 8!), would we have many options?"

"Oh my goodness," Michelle responded, "Plenty!"

"Be specific," I requested.

"Well," she began, "both big boxes are here—both Home Depot and Lowe's are here in Jonesboro and they both sell a ton of flooring." She continued, "Plus, you've got all the national and regional players— Empire Today, Georgia Carpet Outlet—they're all here. And, there are also tons of local independents that would love to put new flooring down for you."

"Wow," I said. "Sounds competitive."

Michelle replied, "Tom, it's cutthroat."

I could feel the seriousness in her tone. I said, "Okay Michelle, if that's the case..." I leaned forward and very deliberately asked, "...then why should we come see you?"

Michelle started, "Tom, you gotta understand, my husband and I started this business 19 years ago. We've got installers that have been with us since day one. These folks know what they're doin'." She proudly stated, "We've got salespeople, some of them have been with us twelve plus years. These folks know what they're talking about!"

After a pause, I said, "Okay Michelle, let me get this straight... you're a flooring store that knows how to sell and install flooring!" (Maybe I wasn't quite that snarky, but close!)

I continued, "I expect when I walk into your showroom, your people can answer my questions. I certainly expect that anyone you send to my home will know what the heck they're doing." I challenged her, "Michelle, what else have you got?"

Michelle defended her answer by telling me about the excellent training she puts her sales team through, she talked about the longevity of the business, and the buying experience she delivers. She offered up a few more reasons to buy from her, none of which were very compelling to me, and I just kept asking, "...and what else? ...and what else?"

Finally, I think more out of frustration than anything, Michelle looked at me and said, "Well, we've got a pretty good guarantee." And with very low expectations, I asked, "Okay, so what's your guarantee?"

Michelle replied, "Tom, if we install your hardwood flooring, you've got sixty days to decide whether or not you love it. If, at any point within those sixty days, you look down and say, 'Aaaaah! We goofed. I can't live with this!' You call me. I'll come out to your home, rip it up, and replace it— free. Installation included."

I sat for a second and I let her answer sink in. Finally, I said, "Wow. That's a pretty darn good guarantee." I asked, "Do you advertise that at all?"

Michelle, sensing I was impressed, looked away and timidly replied, "No, not really."

Like you, Michelle is your typical local advertiser. Smart. Hard working. She puts a high priority on getting her advertising right. But, probably also like you, she's frustrated. She spends good money on advertising every month. A little here, a little there. One message one month, another message the next. Trying to get it right, trying to find the secret sauce, the secret formula so that her advertising will work more often than it doesn't. And it frustrates the heck out of her.

Prior to our meeting in 2009, Michelle was running a campaign on local broadcast television. Her 30-second commercial was a bass thumping, high energy music video style ad that delivered fast-paced images of her inventory with accompanying graphics:

"All carpet on sale now!"

"All hardwoods on sale now!"

"All rugs on sale now!"

"All tile on sale now!"

"Go green with renewable flooring"

"Area rugs from traditional to contemporary"

"Custom-sized stair runners"

"Carpet and ceramic tile cleaning"

Cut to a picture of her delivery truck and her slogan of the month, "Flooring for every budget."

Show phone number and address.

Done.

Yikes. That's what we call "Laundry List Advertising." Feeling the need to include absolutely everything you do into your ad. Shoving the proverbial ten pounds of sugar into the five-pound bag. It was sensory overload, and it wasn't working.

When I came back to see Michelle the following month, I said, "Good news Michelle! We've found your 'one thing', and it's wrapped up in that awesome guarantee of yours." Our revised creative idea for her had a singular focus—what moving forward would now be known as, "The Laws Abbey Flooring Center Sixty Day Walk On It Warranty!" (Credit goes to Phil Bernstein, one of the Jim Doyle & Associates Senior Marketing Consultants, for branding it, "The Sixty Day Walk On It Warranty.")

Strategically, we got Michelle highly targeted on her core. Do you think she knows exactly who her target is? Of course she does! We got her highly focused on exactly who drives her business. In fact, we suggested that Michelle be her own spokesperson because she was a direct reflection of her core customer.

We redirected the budget she was spending on the extremes she was trying to reach. We kept her on broadcast television, but we abandoned her bulk-buy, broad-rotator campaign, and concentrated on the right programming. Yes, it was fewer commercials in fewer programs, but remember, frequently does not equal frequency!

Then, since Michelle's new creative focus was so singular—that awesome guarantee—we were able to use 15-second bookends (splitting a 30-

second commercial into two :15's, placed in the first and last position in the commercial break) and effectively deliver the message with frequency.

In October of 2009, Michelle began her new campaign. She proudly delivered her new message: "Only Laws offers the Abbey Sixty Day Walk On It Warranty. Within sixty days of installation, if you don't like your selection of Abbey tile or hardwood, I'll replace it—FREE. Law's Abbey Flooring Center, 2100 West Washington Avenue, Jonesboro."

By the way, do you remember what the economy was like in 2009? We were in the deepest throws of the Great Recession and every local business in the country was struggling.

So, what happened to sales at Laws Abbey Flooring Center in Jonesboro, AR in October of 2009?

They had one of their best Octobers, ever, with the trend continuing through November and December. Then, in 2010, while every business in the country was hemorrhaging, especially in the home improvement category, Law's Abbey Flooring Center was riding their new campaign from monthly increase to monthly increase. In fact, the campaign worked so well that Michelle decided to extend the corporate-sponsored guarantee on tile and hardwood to include carpeting as well. Today, Law's Abbey Flooring Center is a household name in Jonesboro and surrounding areas, and everyone knows them as home of The Sixty Day Walk on it Warranty.

Here's a quote from Michelle Laws: "Before we met with Jim Doyle & Associates, we thought we needed to be in everything, to get everybody's attention, to reach all the areas we thought we hadn't tapped into. After meeting with them, they advised us to pick a very important category that reaches the audience we need. So, we pulled out of some of our other marketing ventures, partnered more with our television, and it's been very successful. It was almost immediate results.

"I have total strangers that will repeat our commercial and the message that we're presenting. Where before, like every other flooring store out there, we would give our laundry list: we install, we sell floors, we have quality training, we have all these bells and whistles, but nobody remembers that, they expect it, they just kind of fell asleep. So when we paid attention and did the right direction, we had much more measurable success."

Measurable success. How novel is that?

And, because I know you're wondering... the answer is, a few. A few times a year, Michelle has to replace a hardwood floor or a carpet job. But here's the kicker. Michelle is happy to do so! Michelle is smart enough to realize that an unhappy customer does her no good, so she'd rather replace a few flooring jobs each year and have raving fans.

Find your one thing, focus on a singular message, avoid the laundry list.

CHAPTER 14

BRANDING IS OUT, RESULTS ARE IN!

When I titled this book, "Branding is OUT, Results are IN!" I knew it might grab your attention. It is, after all, a bold proclamation, and some of you reading this would probably love to go toe-to-toe with me on it. But allow me to explain by asking a simple question: Have you ever, in your local advertising history, said something like this, *"Well, we advertise just to keep our name out there"*? Or maybe you've said something like, *"Well, we advertise for top of mind awareness."*

I don't know about you, but I haven't met any local advertisers lately who have the patience, nor the budget, to advertise, "Just to keep my name out there." Let's all agree if you're going invest a serious marketing dollar, a precious advertising dollar, that you want to see a very real and very tangible result. Would you agree with me on that? I hope so. So the idea of spending money just "to keep my name out there," frankly, I think is antiquated. I want you to be more deliberate, more strategic, than that. Now, I'm talking about you, as a LOCAL advertiser. If you're Verizon, if you're Apple, if you're Budweiser, if you're a great big national entity with a great big branding budget, then by all means, brand away. But most local advertisers, in the very competitive environment we now live in, need every dollar to deliver a result. That means you need to be a lot more strategic in your advertising.

Now, please, please, please don't misunderstand me. I did NOT say that brands are unimportant. Sometimes my message is misinterpreted. Of course, brands are important. Jim Doyle & Associates is a brand. Everything we do is to protect our brand and grow our brand. Every one of you reading this represents a brand. Some of you wear your brand every day on your apparel. We all understand the value of a brand.

What I am saying is that spending advertising dollars to do nothing more than present your brand—keep your name out there—in the hopes that at some point down the road someone remembers you when they're in your buying cycle, is not enough.

Southwest Airlines. That's a brand. You see that name, you picture their logo, it automatically triggers an idea in your head as to who they are— Southwest Airlines. What does that brand mean to you? Cheap? Low fares? Inexpensive? Those are all in the ballpark. Here is Southwest's brand in four words; *the low-cost airline.* That's it. Everyone knows that if you want to fly cheap, you go Southwest. That's their brand, we can all agree on that.

Now, when you're exposed to Southwest advertising, when Southwest spends good money to convince you and me to choose them over any other airline, what are some of the things they talk about? What's the big campaign that launched Southwest into the stratosphere?

Bags fly FREE!

Does that support Southwest as the low-cost airline? You bet it does! So, while the brand equals low-cost airline, when Southwest advertises, they don't just stop there. They support the brand with a specific offer. Think of other Southwest campaigns, No change fees! $79 One Ways, these are all special offers—dynamic offers—that support the brand and endorse it as the low-cost airline.

Branding is out and results are in. Creating special, dynamic offers moves your advertising from just putting your brand out there to giving your customer an actionable purchase decision.

Let me make the point a little more dramatically with this example of two auto repair franchises located in two different markets. Same franchise, same logo, same jingle. Each embarks on an early summer advertising campaign to support air-conditioning checks. After reading these two scripts, which one do you think drove more cars to the shop on Saturday?

Franchise A:

Owner as Spokesperson: "Hi, I'm Mike Jones, your Car Doctor guy! Let's talk about keeping your vehicle running trouble free, and saving you money! Your vehicle may not be cool on the outside, but we'll keep it cool on the inside. Our guys are trained, tested, and top of the line. They'll get your vehicle in, diagnose the problem, let you know the best way to solve it, and have you back on the road... calm, cool and comfortable. Full service, great value. Come to Car Doctor."

Jingle out: "...don't worry, call the Car Doctor!"

Franchise B:

Female Customer: "My car may not be coolest on the outside, but this summer I want it cool on the inside... real cool!"

Announcer: "Cool off with a full a/c performance check, just $29.99 only at Car Doctor!"

Jingle out: "...don't worry call the Car Doctor!"

Now, if you're sitting on your sofa during the dog days of summer and you know your car air conditioning isn't cranking the way you want it to, which of these two gets you to the shop on Saturday? Franchise A? Mr. "Full service, great value!" Or, Franchise B? Mr. "$29.99, bring it in, we'll figure out what's wrong."

I contend Franchise B's creative, with an offer, is dramatically more effective. Branding is out, results are in for the local advertiser.

Here's my fear. My fear is that some of you reading this right now are thinking, "Yeah, but we're not retail, so we can't do an offer." Or you're thinking, "My category of business really doesn't lend itself to having an offer." Or worse yet, you're thinking, "Well, all you're saying to do is discount... and we don't discount!"

That's not what I'm saying. I'm saying support your brand with an offer in your advertising that your prospect can act on. Don't just promise full service and great value, support it with a $29.99 performance check! Don't just promise low airfares, support it with free baggage or $79 one way tickets! Create a dynamic offer that will knock your prospect's socks off. And it doesn't have to be price related. The "Sixty Day Walk on it Warranty" has nothing to do with price, and Law's Abbey Flooring Center isn't the discount flooring store in Jonesboro.

Let me give you some more examples of categories that you might not immediately think of as being "offer friendly," but with a little thought, easily lend themselves to an offer. For example, how about a hospital. Now what kind of an offer can a hospital have? Well, how about this: The Fifteen Minute ER Guarantee!

"At Mercy General Hospital, we guarantee from the moment you walk through our ER doors that you will be addressed by a healthcare professional within fifteen minutes or less!"

It's a dynamic offer that eliminates the biggest objection to going to the ER, I don't want to sit there all day!

How about this category: Law firms. What kind of offer can a law firm have? What about: Walk In Wednesdays!

"Do you think you have a reason to speak to an attorney? Walk in any Wednesday, no appointment necessary, no fee... and you will speak with an attorney."

Every Wednesday, the firm could create an "up" system for their attorneys, like a car dealership, and watch brand new faces walk in the door. Now, their advertising has become measurable! Think about that. "Gee, we advertised over there for the first half of the year and averaged six new faces every Wednesday. We moved our advertising over here for the second half of the year and now we're down to two new faces. We should probably move our advertising back over there, since it worked better." Now you'd know.

Again, I understand the power of branding and believe in the concept of brands, however, I am uncomfortable when I see a local landscape company use their ad dollars to try to create a brand without trying to sell something specific. I see way too many, "When it comes to all your landscaping needs, call Green Thumb Landscaping. We Do It Right" ads. The branding message runs with no offer, no call to action, and no reason for a homeowner to pick up the phone and call today. I see way too many local advertisers, be they landscapers, furniture stores, car dealerships, restaurants, etc., spend precious ad dollars on branding messages that fail to ask consumers to do something.

Most advertisers are just branding around doing nothing. They just brand there, with everyone else, hoping that something good happens.

And one of the negative side effects of branding-only campaigns is the inability to connect ad dollars to results. Mr. Green Thumb Landscaping may or may not get calls from his message, and it will be really hard for him to connect any type of ROI to his campaign. At least with a results-oriented message that has an offer with a deadline, he can tell whether or not he sold something from his efforts.

Here's my analogy. Consider two friends, Jeff and Mike. Both work for the same company and are assigned to work a trade show booth together. At the trade show, Jeff is active, approachable, energetic and makes it a point to introduce himself around even outside of their booth. Jeff has "Buy one Get one" coupons printed and hands them out aggressively. Mike, at the same booth, just brands around, waiting for people to approach him. When a few do approach, he's nice and describes his company and their product and tells them to call him when they're ready. Which employee is leaving the show with more leads?

Don't just brand there, do something...

CHAPTER 15

POINT OF ENTRY

There is an often overlooked piece of the local advertising puzzle that we call your POE—Point of Entry.

Your point of entry is defined as, "What is it that most first-timers are interested in?" This can be a critical element to the success of your advertising. Again, why do most local businesses spend money on advertising? To get new customers/clients/patients. So, let's identify what the newbie is most interested in, and then highlight it in your creative message.

If you're in a category with a clear-cut point of entry product or service, identifying it and highlighting it can be the difference between advertising that works and advertising that doesn't. Unfortunately, many local advertisers shy away from focusing on their point of entry, oftentimes because it's not their sexiest product or service. For example, I once met with a podiatrist and told her I wanted to make her "The Bunion

Specialist"! She looked at me like I had two heads. She said, "Do you know how long I went to school to be a podiatrist? And you want me to be the bunion specialist?" She definitely didn't hide her disappointment in my creative suggestion.

I defended my suggestion. "Do you remember our conversation when I was diagnosing your business?" I asked. "My question was, if you see a brand-new patient—someone you've never seen in your office before—why are they there? You said, 'It's always one of two things. Either they have an ingrown toenail, or they have a bunion.' In fact, you went on to tell me that more than one third of all American women have bunions, mainly because of the types of shoes they wear. Well, if there's this great big population out there, and it's what brings most new patients to you, why wouldn't you be, The Bunion Specialist?" This particular podiatrist certainly didn't see herself focusing on bunions in her practice, but if it's what leads to a healthy business and increased patient base, it's worth strong consideration.

Why is the Point of Entry so critical? For a couple of reasons. First, most advertising is designed to acquire new customers. Almost every advertiser spends in order to drive new customers. So, if we can define which product or service brings in most new customers, that would potentially be the focus of the creative.

Secondly, it helps us get to the bigger sale. My colleague, Don Fitzgibbons, the Guru of Ads, defines point of entry this way. He says, "If you want to sell parrots, advertise parakeets. Why? Because everyone who bought a one-thousand-dollar parrot, bought a forty-dollar parakeet first!" In fact, I once shared Don's POE definition in a local advertising seminar, and at the end of my session an audience member came barreling up the center aisle, got right in front of me and said, "I own a pet store, I'll give ya the darn parakeet!"

In the furniture category, a classic point of entry product is the recliner. Every furniture store owner would love to sell multi-thousand-dollar dining room sets all day. However, a potentially better new customer driver is the recliner.

I was touring a local furniture store in a small town in Wisconsin, with the owner, peppering him with my usual questions. Finally, I asked, "If you see a new face in your store—someone who has never been here before—and they buy something, what do they buy?"

He immediately replied, "That's easy. They buy a recliner."

"Okay," I said, and then dug deeper. "Do you have a lot of recliners in stock?"

He pointed to the next room and said, "That room right there, that's my recliner gallery. I've got nothing but recliners in there."

We entered his gallery, and as I overlooked what appeared to be a sea of recliners, I asked, "Whattya got in here, like 50 recliners?"

"Oh, more than that!" he answered.

"Sixty?" I guessed.

"More than that" he said.

"Seventy?" I estimated.

"Probably more than that. I figure on any given day, I have over 80 recliners on the floor to choose from," he said.

Bingo! We not only identified his point of entry, but we also discovered his one thing! A great selection of recliners drives plenty of new faces and a claim of "Always 80 on the floor" establishes a position—a Unique Selling Proposition—an identity in the market that separates him from every other furniture store in town.

When I brought back the "Always 80 recliners on the floor" idea, the store owner was a bit reluctant to plant his flag solely in one item. He had plenty of other inventory under his roof that needed to be sold. I explained that in advertising, "a rising tide brings up all ships," meaning, if he singularly focused on recliners and drove new faces through his doors, he'd experience an increase across all his departments. It took a little bit to convince him, but once I had, he embraced my recommendation. His very first version of the creative had him wearing a #80 Green Bay Packers jersey, proudly announcing, "Leather recliners, swivel recliners, double recliners, reclining sofas, and more. We always have 80 recliners on the floor to choose from, starting at just $299."

His "Always 80 recliners on the floor to choose from" became a homerun campaign.

In your business, do you have a clear-cut point of entry product or service? Can you easily answer, "What is it that most first-timers are interested in?" The point of entry concept is so important that it's worth doing a bit of research within your organization. Go back and review the last 100 new customer or new client or new patient interactions. What does the data reveal? Review your first visit website traffic. What patterns do you see? Can you identify a point of entry strategy?

I'll tell you one category killer that gets the point of entry concept, Guitar Center. Guitar Centers are a musician's playground. I love walking into a Guitar Center anywhere in the country and seeing and hearing musicians of all levels banging away on instruments. But, take a close look at Guitar Center advertising and you'll discover that most of their attention is on the beginner. They're masters at introductory packages that include things like guitar, amp, strap, picks, tuner and a "learn to play" CD, all for under $200! I'm a Guitar Center customer and I get plenty of Guitar Center direct mail. The front cover features are almost always lower end beginner offers, especially before the holidays!

One additional word of caution, though. Point of entry does not always mean "Entry Level." Be careful not to confuse the two. For example, for the Harley Davidson dealer who wants to sell more new bikes, the entry level Harley may NOT be the point of entry. Men between the ages of 40 and 50 who are rewarding themselves with a new Harley aren't interested in the entry level model. Even though they're new to Harley, they won't waste time with a smaller model, they'll go right for the HOG in the showroom!

CHAPTER 16

TOM'S CREATIVE FORMULA

Do you want a default branding template you can use for your next ad that WON'T WORK! Here ya go, free from me to you...

Hey (insert city here).

For all your (insert category here) needs, call (insert client name here)!

For over (insert # of years in business) years, (insert client name) has been helping (insert city) with all your (insert category) needs.

Our expert staff ...

Quality...

Customer service...

When you're ready...

(Insert client name)... (slogan that doesn't offer a value proposition).

There you have it—knock yourself out. It's pretty much the default script that every (un)creative director or script writer at your local media outlet uses when they (and you) have no clue why someone should choose you over anyone else in your competitive landscape, and it won't work.

When it comes time for me to sit down and craft a message for a local advertiser, I have a specific creative formula I use.

USP + POE (triggers and questions) + offer/call-to-action = RESULTS

Now, I'd like to tell you that every piece of creative I've ever written follows this formula perfectly, but that's just not the case. It's more of a guide than an absolute. There are things, as you'll see below, that I strive to include in each piece of creative I write, however, sometimes I don't get all of the elements included.

Here's how I go about crafting a message. Picture a big, empty creative bucket in front of me. The first thing I drop in the bucket is your USP, your Unique Selling Proposition, your "one thing." That's going in the bucket first, and is the thing that will anchor our creative, which is why correctly identifying your "one thing" is so important.

The second thing I drop in the bucket is your POE—Point of Entry. If the advertiser has a clear-cut point of entry and I've made sure to uncover it, that goes in the bucket next. If our goal is to deliver new faces, then it's important to explore what most first-timers are interested in.

The third thing I add are any triggers that lead

to the first interaction with your prospect. Are there very specific events or common circumstances that many of your first-time prospects experience that have motivated them to take action? If so, show those triggers in the creative so when it finally happens to the consumer, they know what they're supposed to do! And, if you already know their concerns, answer their questions so you can begin to build a relationship with your prospect through your creative. When you anticipate what they want to know and answer that in your creative, the consumer feels like you're inside their head! And, if you don't want to give all of your information away in your creative, at least tease that you know the answers. Maybe drive them to a website to learn more.

Finally, I include a good strong offer with a call to action.

If I can get all these elements in my creative bucket, no matter how I stir it up and paint it out the other side, I'm well on my way to a RESULTS-oriented piece of creative. I take your one thing, I add it to your first thing, I surround it with those triggers and questions, and I knock your socks off with a strong offer with a deadline. Get all that in the bucket, and we're gonna rock.

USP + POE (triggers and questions) + offer/call-to-action = RESULTS

Here's an example...

Hometown Furniture. What's their one thing? They always have 101 recliners on the floor to choose from. It's not the beautiful showroom. It's not the friendly, knowledgeable staff. What do they claim that no one else in town claims? 101 recliners always in stock.

What's their point of entry? Recliners. A new face might not drop a few grand on a bedroom set on their first visit to Hometown Furniture, but they can and will load a new recliner in the back of their pickup, SUV or mini-van.

What's the trigger to a recliner purchase? There are many, including a move, the start of football season, or even getting ready for holiday gatherings.

What questions does a newbie have? Do you have a good selection? How much? How soon can I get it home? Financing?

Create an offer and give it a deadline.

My creative might be: *"It's our massive End of Summer blowout at Hometown Furniture, where you'll always find 101 recliners on the floor to choose from! From leather recliners to swivel recliners to reclining sofas and more, we always have 101 recliners in stock, ready for immediate delivery. And right now, just in time for the start of the football season, the whole family can enjoy the game from this Lane, double reclining sofa.*

Regularly $899, just $599 during our End of Summer blowout. Load it up and take it home or let us deliver FREE! Hurry in, sale ends Saturday. The massive end of summer blowout, now through Saturday, only at Hometown Furniture, where you'll always find 101 recliners to choose from."

Award winning? Heck no! Effective? Absolutely. In fact, we worked with a furniture store owner in the Midwest who came to one of my advertising seminars and decided to plant their flag in "101 recliners." They got singular with their message and got highly targeted to their core. Within eight months they reported a 60% increase in sales.

Diagnose your one thing. Find your point of entry. Identify your triggers. Determine the common questions every newbie wants to know. Create an astounding offer. Have a call-to-action. Earn results.

CHAPTER 17

KEEP IT SIMPLE

I had to laugh when I was thumbing through a magazine aimed at healthy living for the aging Baby Boomer. When you live in Sarasota, Florida, these magazines have a way of sneaking into your life!

I was intrigued by the many ads in the magazine and I came across an ad for a local vision center. The ad focused on cataract surgery, specifically a product called Crystalens. There, in full color, was Mrs. Carol Brady herself—Florence Henderson. She was spokesperson for Crystalens (and a real Crystalens patient!). The ad was simple and clean, and featured this quote from Ms. Henderson, "Life shouldn't look like an old rerun. That's why I chose the cataract replacement lens that corrects more than just cataracts."

Crystalens, the cataract replacement lens that fixes more than just cataracts.

The subtext simply stated: Crystalens is the only replacement lens that corrects both your cataracts and your full range of vision, so you can see near, far, and everywhere in between.

A simple, easy to understand, effective USP.

When I turned the page, I encountered another ad for a different cataract and laser institute, clearly a direct competitor of the vision center on the previous page. There was a nice picture of the local doctor and copy that touted him as, "a Refractive Cataract Surgeon with extensive experience in multifocal, accommodative, and astigmatic intra-ocular lenses."

What!? Multifocal, accommodative, and astigmatic intraocular what?

Look, I'm sure the good doctor is a highly skilled healthcare provider, but his advertising needs some help! I doubt anyone has ever walked into his office and said, "I'm interested in your multifocal astigmatic intraocular lenses..." But I could easily imagine someone requesting, "Those Mrs. Brady cataract lenses that fix more than just my cataracts..."

Here's a little copywriting rule I live by. If you type a word in your script, and Microsoft Word underlines it in red because they've never heard it, it's probably not a good word to use in your creative (i.e. "intraocular").

When it comes to copy, write it like you'd tell it to a friend. Keep the jargon to a minimum. Use simple words.

Winston Churchill said that "short words are best and the old words, when short, are best of all." And my favorite quote on simple words...

"*I love words, but I don't like strange ones. You don't understand them and they don't understand you. Old words is like old friends, you know 'em the minute you see 'em.*" -Will Rogers

Keep your copy simple.

CHAPTER 18

BUYTHEHOLE.COM

Another big creative mistake we see all the time is advertising that focuses on the drill bit, not the hole. One of the oldest clichés in business school is "sell the hole, not the drill bit." Basically, it means that thousands of times a day, American consumers walk into a hardware store and buy a quarter inch drill bit. But what do they really want? They want a quarter inch hole. The drill bit is nothing more than the tool that delivers the desired end result.

The big creative mistake so many local advertisers make is they focus on the drill bit—their tool—and ignore the consumers desired end result. Here are some classic examples we still see all the time...

The dentist's ad showing someone poking and probing around in a patient's mouth. Nobody wants that! Nobody goes to the dentist because we enjoy the experience. We go because we want a healthy smile. Or we go to get relief from pain. I don't want to see images of someone scraping, tapping, tugging or drilling.

I crack up every time I see a laser hair removal ad that shows someone with a surgeon's mask and a face shield, that looks like it came off a welder's helmet, going to work on a laid out patient who has to wear eye protection to avoid getting their retina scorched. That's not what she wants. She wants her friends to tell her she looks great. She wants her husband to show her affection like he hasn't shown in years. That's what she wants from her laser hair removal experience.

It's the auto service center that insists on showing the mechanic under the hood. It's the roofing company that feels compelled to show workers nail-gunning shingles. Those are drill bit images, not holes. Don't focus on the tools or technology, focus on the motivation and emotion.

And, once you've figured out your hole, buy "the hole.com."

If you can clearly figure out your hole—what the customer is really buying—can you add a dotcom and buy that domain name?

Let me give an example. A few years ago, one of our Senior Marketing Consultants, Perry Kapiloff, met with a landscape company with an unusually long name. Perry uncovered that their "hole"— what they were really selling—was great looking lawns. So, Perry assisted them in securing the domain, "www.greatlookinglawns.com" and built an entire campaign around their hole. He helped them to "buythehole.com."

Here's a different example. Say you're a local self-storage facility and you know that your real target is women who hate all their husband's stuff cluttering the garage. What's your customer really buying? Storage? Well, I guess, but is that really what she wants? Doesn't she really just want her garage back? Imagine a campaign targeting her with a call to action to learn more about your facility at "www.givemebackmygarage.com"!

Remember Johnson's Baby Shampoo. What was their hole, what were they selling? Beautiful hair for kids? Nope, they were selling a shampoo that wouldn't sting if it got into the eyes of little ones. They were selling "No more tears." Guess who owns "www.nomoretears.com"? That's right, Johnson's Baby Shampoo bought the hole.com.

CHAPTER 19

OWN THE DOMAIN TO OWN THE POSITION

Let's face it, your website is your new front door, and has been for some time now. Having a strong Internet presence at your website is a must. And, while we're talking about it, you better make sure your site is mobile-optimized. Today, more searches happen on a mobile device than on a desktop, which is why, in April of 2015, Google made a major change to its algorithm punishing websites that are not mobile friendly.

One of the first steps to a decent Internet presence is securing a URL that makes sense. Over my many years of traveling the country working with local advertisers, and even before that in my years with an Internet development company, I've seen lots of businesses struggle with understanding this first step. (For the life of me, I still can't understand why so many law firms insisted on separating names in their URL with a hyphen!) Many early adopters were smart enough to secure their actual business name as their URL, typically a very smart move. However, if your business name is easily misspelled or your actual business name is not how the market refers to you, it can be a challenge. Using hyphens, .net's, .biz's, or hard to spell names are all symptoms of businesses that are "domain name challenged."

If you're lucky enough to have an easily understood business name that's the recognized way the market refers to you, and you were smart enough to secure that as your URL, good for you.

Smithford.com
Sarasotakitchenandbath.com
Precisiongaragedoor.com
Gallowdental.com
Southeastplumbing.com
Owenheatingandcooling.com
Morganlaw.com
ToyotaofOrchardPark.com
Riversidefurniture.com...

These are all simple business names that would have some level of familiarity in their respective markets and are fine domain names. No problem.

The challenge is with the many, many businesses that aren't fortunate enough to have a simple, easily understood, easy to spell, easy to remember business name. If the website is your new front door, and your URL is your address, you'd better get it right!

Choosing the proper domain is part art and

part science, and there are plenty of online tools designed to help discover a great domain (simply Google "domain name help" and you'll be presented with a number of different tools and services).

Each time I diagnose a business to help with their local advertising, I make a decision about their URL from a marketing perspective. I need to decide pretty early on if their domain is one that will work for advertising purposes or if we need to find a better option. If I determine that a business is "domain name challenged," one of my first default strategies is to see if I can help them own a domain in order to own a position.

Own the domain to own the position. As you work to plant your flag and own a position in a marketplace, see if you can secure that position as a URL. For example, if you want to be known as your city's place to go for barbeque, you might own, mytownbestbbq.com. If you want to be the first name someone thinks of when it comes to divorce in your city, own mytowndivorce.com.

Imagine you're criminal defense attorney, Bill Robinson, in Tucson, AZ, and you want to dominate the DUI defense category. You don't own the domain robinsonlaw.com because some other attorney named Robinson, somewhere else in the world, has already captured it. So you settled on Robinson-law.com as your domain. Not a terrible domain, but not a great one either because that hyphen is going to cost you visitors. If you want to be Tucson's DUI guy, secure the domain, "Tucsonduiguy.com"! Imagine the singularly focused campaign that has the ability to drive traffic to Tucsonduiguy.com. *"Hi, I'm attorney Bill Robinson. Do you count your money when it comes out of the ATM? Of course, you do! Why? Well, because you know sometimes machines make mistakes. If you've been arrested for DUI and have failed a field breathalyzer, call me because I know that the courts know, that sometimes machines make mistakes! If you've been arrested for DUI, call me, I'm Attorney Bill Robinson, Tucson's DUI guy. Visit tucsonduiguy.com!"*

Own the domain to own the position.

I love the strategy of Massey Auto, the used car, high credit-risk dealer in Eugene, Oregon, who owns the domain, www.messycredit.com. The creative for all of his advertising focuses on his ability to get anyone approved with a call to action to go to messycredit.com. No pricing, no specific inventory, just a straight-forward message with a specific call to action.

In Sarasota, Florida every restaurant battles to claim the best grouper sandwich in town. When I first moved here, I had a friend come visit. I said, "Dave, what do you want to do when you arrive?" He said, "Tom, I'd like to get an ice cold beer and a grouper sandwich!" Not yet familiar with the local restaurant scene, I asked my wife to find us a place to take our visitor. Upon Dave's arrival we went directly to a terrific waterfront hangout called The Beach House. Midway through an awesome grouper sandwich, I turned to my wife and asked, "So how did you find this place?" Of course she replied, "I Googled "grouper sandwich Sarasota" and they came up." Guess what URL The Beach House owns? "www.groupersandwich.com"! I suppose if you want to claim the best grouper sandwich on earth, you own the domain to own the position.

For the personal injury attorney in Kansas City, who only wanted serious injury cases, we advised, "KCseriousinjuryattorney.com." For the used car dealer in Buffalo, who wanted to plant his flag in trucks, we recommended Buffalotruckking.com. For a podiatrist, whom we advised to focus on bunions, we suggested bunionrelief.com. For Dr. Keith, the chiropractor with an incredibly long last name, we recommended, drkeithpainrelief.com. For the John Deere dealer who wanted to focus on leasing, we suggested leaseadeere.com.

If your advertising is going to claim that you own a particular position and you can back it up by owning that position via your URL, well, who's going to dispute that? "They must have the best grouper sandwich, they own it on the world wide web!"

Own the domain to own the position.

CHAPTER 20

CREATE **KOHL**OSSAL EVENTS!

I came upon an ad for a local pizzeria. The ad was okay, not great. It talked about their great product. But then again, don't they *all* claim the BEST product? It had an offer—a large pizza for nine dollars and ninety-nine cents. I don't know what pizza sells for in your market, but to me, $9.99 for a large pizza sounded just okay, it didn't sound like an amazing offer.

Here's the big problem I had with the ad. There was no deadline! And with no deadline, the offer sounded lame. It gave me the sense that $9.99 was the everyday price. The copy didn't even say, "For a limited time only!" It actually said, "...and now get a large pizza for $9.99..." There was no sense of urgency, no parameters or boundaries to the offer to give me the feeling that this was a special price, just "now." Seemingly, I could "get a pizza for $9.99" for however long their ad budget lasted.

In the restaurant category, they call them LTO's—Limited Time Offers. And they work. The whole idea behind the LTO is that this special price won't last, so you'd better hurry up and act. I once had an owner of a national sandwich franchise tell me it didn't matter what the product was, if they said it was available for a limited time only, they'd sell a ton of product. This demonstrates the power of a deadline.

Deadlines do several things...

First, a deadline creates urgency. A deadline can take a prospect from a "maybe, sometime soon" buyer to an action taking prospect. There has to be some fear of loss, and a deadline helps create that.

Secondly, a deadline helps determine ROI. A deadline gives the advertiser a better opportunity to measure results. It's much easier to know whether a campaign worked when there's a specific offer with a deadline as opposed to a branding campaign or a weak offer with no expiration.

Finally, a deadline forces a buying decision. Will I make this purchase by this time? Without a deadline, the consumer isn't forced into making a yes/no decision because doing nothing and not missing out is still an option.

Deadlines and astonishing offers are part of what I call creating KOHLossal events.

You're certainly familiar with retail giant, KOHL's. I think KOHL's gets it when it comes to creating high sense of urgency, fear of loss campaigns. Through their strategies of using super high frequency campaigns that tout big, big discounts in a short window of opportunity, they create KOHLossal events.

With Kohl's, it's all about big savings—forty, fifty, even sixty percent or more—but for a very limited time, such as this weekend only!

Kohl's has become the master of things like Early Bird savings, Door Buster specials, Late Night events, Power Hours. They're all high urgency, astonishing offers in a limited window of opportunity. And they work. Who hasn't heard someone say, "I've got ten dollars worth of Kohl's cash that I have to spend this weekend!"

I think we can all learn a lesson from Kohl's. The next time you want to spread your limited budget across a whole month and offer a paltry ten or fifteen percent discount, consider creating a KOHLossal event. Take that same budget, run it over three or four days, and create an outrageous offer that will turn heads.

Instead of $9.99 pizzas anytime, make it 2 for $10.00 on Tuesdays only!

Rather than 15% off all month, make it 40% this Saturday from 9a to 12p only!

And then, instead of asking yourself at the end of the month, "Did it work?" and thinking, "Aaah, I don't know," you can stand in your showroom on a Saturday and watch the best day of the quarter unfold, because you created a KOHLossal event.

CHAPTER 21

HAVE A CHICKEN LITTLE IN YOUR AD!

We all know the story about Chicken Little, the poor fowl who got bopped on the head by an acorn and then ran around warning: "The sky is falling, the sky is falling!" As Chicken Little encounters each of his barnyard buddies, he insists, "I saw it with my own eyes and heard it with my own ears, and part of it fell on my head!" Through his drama, sense of urgency and utter belief in his experience, Chicken Little manages to convince Henny Penny, Loosey Goosey, Ducky Lucky, and Turkey Lurkey that they must immediately run and tell the King.

What's the lesson of this old fable? One source I read said the lesson is, "Courage. Don't be afraid. The sky is not falling." Another source said the moral is, "Don't believe everything you're told." In fact, Chicken Little Syndrome is described as fear-mongering!

You want to know what my take-away is from this story? Have a call to action with a sense of urgency!

I say, have a Chicken Little in every ad. Imagine a character in your advertising that is so dramatic, so convincing, so hell-bent on immediate action that they could whip everyone they encountered into a believing frenzy! Isn't that the objective of the creative—to deliver a message that prompts the masses into immediate action?

Car dealers and furniture stores are great at this. Really good automotive and furniture advertisers whip us into a buying frenzy through their belief and a message that right now is the absolute best time to buy.

In upstate New York, and now in South Florida, the nation's biggest seller of Hyundai's, Billy Fuccillo, is a mainstay on television. He can be seen regularly on broadcast and cable TV touting the benefits of buying a new Hyundai or Kia. Billy owns a word in his markets. It's "HUUUUUUUUUGE!"

Billy Fuccillo is also an amazing Chicken Little! In every ad, he is so convincing that "Right now is the very best time to buy..." He masterfully plays on current events and factors to create a sense of urgency. A typical Billy Fuccillo ad might say, "Folks, there will never be a better time to buy than right now. Gas prices are going up again and these new Hyundai fuel-efficient vehicles are the answer...." Or, "Interest rates are at a record low, new models are coming in, and I just promised the factory I'd sell 500 new vehicles by the end of the month. I gotta move these cars right now!" Whatever is current is his acorn to the head—rising gas prices, falling gas prices, snow storms, tax season, inflation, deflation, bad economy, good economy, tough lending standards, loosening lending standards—whatever the current situation, Ol' Chicken Little Billy will figure a way to shout, "The sky is falling" and convince the masses that right now is the absolute best time to buy.

One final note: As dramatic and convincing as Billy is with a sense of urgency, he always ties his Sky is Falling message in with a WIIFM. There is always a "What's In It For Me" for the customer.

Sky is Falling	WIIFM
Rising gas prices	Fuel-efficient vehicles available to lower your monthly gas cost
Easing credit from the banks	We can get you bought
Snow storm	Too much inventory piled up, so we're dealing

Every month, Billy has a compelling reason as to why right now is the very best time to buy, and why it benefits the customer. Go to Youtube and search "Billy Fuccillo commercials," and watch a few to see how he does it. And, before you turn up your nose and say, "Oh I would never run something like that!" consider the elements of his creative: triggers to buy, high sense of urgency, great offer, call to action with a deadline, and a consistent word that he absolutely owns... Huuuuuuuuuuge!

Granted, I'm pretty sure a Fuccillo commercial has never won an Addy, but I'm also pretty sure Billy doesn't care.

CHAPTER 22

WRITE YOUR ADS TO BE PULLED!

H ave you ever had to call your media partner in a panic and tell them to PULL THE AD! I hope so. Usually when a client calls with this demand, the ad is working so well that the client can't fulfill the offer anymore.

Pull the ad, the tickets are all sold!

Pull the ad, I don't have any cars left to sell!

Pull the ad, the 4-piece stainless steel kitchen special worked so well, I'm out of inventory!

That's what we want to happen—campaigns that work so well the client sells out.

I once worked with an appliance store owner who told me, "I use newspaper to hammer price, I use TV and radio to hammer the tradition of my business." What do you think this guy answered when I asked him, "Of all of your media, what works best?" Of course, he said, "Newspaper!" No one will ever say, "Pull the ads! You're overselling the tradition of my business!" It's NEVER happened and it never will.

So, write your ads to be pulled. Write them with a specific offer so great, you get overrun with customers. Write them with an offer so astonishing you have customers fighting over it. Write them so that results will be so dramatic you'll have to pull the ad.

Now, moving forward, apply this test. When you're done with your script, re-read the ad and ask yourself, "Does it have the potential to be pulled?" If not, you probably haven't crafted the best ad.

CHAPTER 23

WEAK OFFER, WEAK RESULTS. SPECTACULAR OFFER, SPECTACULAR RESULTS

What has the greatest effect on whether an ad will work? It might just be the offer. Here's my plea. If you're going to invest in an advertising campaign, push yourself beyond your comfort zone on the offer.

Weak offer, weak results. Spectacular offer, spectacular results.

The more dramatic your offer—the more outrageous, astounding and incredible the offer—the more it will turn heads, capture attention and generate buzz throughout your customer base. As a secondary effect, it will also create more excitement among your own staff. When I tell an audience of local advertisers about Michelle Laws, I literally hear "oohs" and "aahs" erupt when I reveal the "Sixty Day Walk on it Warranty." That offer turns heads, that offer creates a buzz, and that offer galvanized her entire staff toward a mission they could all get behind. That offer works!

119

Don't simply create an offer just to have an offer, make it worth something. And don't mistake an offer with standard practice. If every replacement window company in your market does free estimates, then "free estimates" is not an offer! If every cosmetic med spa in town does the initial consultation for free, then "free consultation" is not an offer! At least not an amazing offer.

While listening to a sports talk show, I heard the host do a live read for a local lawn service. He said, "And right now, sign up for five lawn treatments and after the fifth treatment, we'll send out one of our professional lawn inspectors to do a full lawn assessment for FREE!" Okay, let me get this straight. I pay you to send out a guy to treat my lawn five times, and then you'll send the expert to do an assessment? Shouldn't you have sent the expert to do the assessment first? And, if you've done five treatments, my lawn had better be in great shape! What kind of offer is that?

Remember the incredible success of the Denny's Free Grand Slam Breakfast promotion in the Super Bowl? It was a fantastic example of having an outrageous offer, with a deadline, that simply rocked. To refresh your memory, Denny's invested in the biggest national advertising platform ever created, the Super Bowl in order to take back share. They focused on their best-seller, the Grand Slam. They created an astonishing offer—free. And, they created a sense of urgency—this Tuesday from 6a to 2p only. They also created lines out their door and tremendous marketing buzz!

Denny's Formula:
Big spend during challenging times: to gain share
Great Platform: The Super Bowl
Spectacular Offer: FREE
With a Deadline: Tuesday only from 6am to 2pm

This formula was put to the test again sometime later by KFC (Kentucky Fried Chicken) and it passed with flying colors.

The KFC promotion!
Oprah Winfrey announced on her show that coupons for a free Kentucky grilled chicken dinner would be available on her website.

The demand was so overwhelming that KFC struggled to accommodate everyone.

According to KFC, the company has never had such a response to a special-meal offer. "It's unprecedented in our more than 50 years," a KFC spokesperson told the AP at the time. "It beats anything we've ever done."

The Formula:
Big spend during challenging times: to gain share
Great Platform: Oprah
Astonishing Offer: FREE
With a Deadline: This Wednesday only

FREE is one of the most powerful words in

121

advertising. If you want to drive sampling of a new product, FREE is a great way to get started. But, don't be confused. Free hot dogs is not an enticement to a $35,000 new car purchase. Free estimates and free consultations in categories where everybody does free estimates and consultations are not spectacular offers. If you don't like your new flooring, we'll replace it FREE, now that's a spectacular offer.

There's a local advertiser in Central Florida (the Tampa and Orlando markets) who dominates a category—mortgage lending. Robert Palmer is the man behind RP Funding. In a category that typically isn't very "noisy," Palmer is a standout.

He has carved his niche with outstanding offers like:

- *We don't charge any lender fees "because you shouldn't have to pay to get a mortgage"*
- *$1,000 Guarantee – If you receive a legitimate offer from a competitor that is lower, our promise to you is that we will match it, and if we can't, we'll give you $1,000*
- *10 Day Accelerated Closing Program*
- *"I'll pay ALL of your closing costs to re-finance"*

Palmer ran a campaign that included a word that caught my attention: "disrupting." The creative open goes something like, "I'm Robert Palmer, and I'm disrupting the mortgage lending category..."

As a professional marketer, I appreciate the

power in this word. It signals that Palmer has discovered new and better techniques that are shaking up old-school tactics. Once he introduces himself as a disruptor, he follows with a specific offer like, "No lender fees because you shouldn't have to pay to get a mortgage!" This makes a powerful position and statement.

One spectacular offer that's resonating with today's consumer is speed. We've had tremendous success using a "call us this morning, we will see you TODAY!" strategy across a number of different categories.

We discovered the concept while working with a chiropractor in Texas. He told us that he leaves appointment time available every day to take care of emergencies. We came back with a strategy to run short 15-second commercials on television in overnights and early morning news. The message was simple. For the overnights, the ad said, "Can't sleep because you're in pain? Call me this morning, I will see you TODAY!" For the morning news, it was, "Did you wake up in pain? Call me this morning, I will see you TODAY!"

The campaign took off immediately. We've successfully replicated this strategy in various markets, and we've expanded it to numerous other categories, including dental and OB/GYN. We've adapted the strategy for home services like HVAC, plumbing, and garage door service. "Air conditioning won't work...," "Got a leaking faucet...," "Garage door broken... call us this morning, we will see you TODAY!"

Whether it's an awesome discount, incredible speed or an astonishing guarantee, push yourself to create a spectacular offer. Weak offer, weak results. Spectacular offer, spectacular results.

CHAPTER 24

SUNDAY, SUNDAY, SUNDAY!

Many local campaigns are designed around events, be it a big sale, a gathering like a festival or concert, or trying to fill seats at an educational, medical or financial seminar.

Everything I know about executing event style advertising I learned from one of my earliest clients back in my radio days. Each January, I handled the monster truck show event. The promoter was a guy out of Ohio, named Aaron, and he taught me more about how to advertise an event than any other experience I've ever had.

Every winter, Aaron would bring his indoor motorsports show to please the snowbound crowds throughout the Northeast. He'd deliver thrills from trucks named Bigfoot, Gravedigger, and Excalibur. One year he brought the Human Bomb, a guy who would climb in a box with dynamite and blow himself up. The crowd loved it. One year, he brought a jet-powered four-wheeler, and the audience watched with amazement as a guy sat atop a jet engine, flame-throwing ATV. The louder, the smellier, the hotter, the better!

Aaron was a master promoter and each year he'd sell out hockey barns and auditoriums full of satisfied fans. When I first started working with Aaron, i.e. selling him advertising, I thought I knew how to promote an event. I quickly learned that I was the student and Aaron was the teacher.

Here are the 3 top lessons he taught me in event promotion...

1) Pick the right vehicles and dominate. Aaron's plan called for one television partner and one radio partner, that's it. He knew exactly who his target was, so he'd identify the best radio and TV outlet in each market to reach that target, and forge a partnership. He knew his budget would give him some clout, so he'd choose his partners carefully. Then, along with his aggressive ad schedule, he'd create additional promotional opportunities where the media partner could generate additional revenues. One year, I sold a sponsorship to his show to the local Chevy dealer association and had the Chevrolet monster truck appear at various dealerships. Aaron resisted the temptation to "spread it around."

2) Concentrate the campaign. Aaron's plan went something like this:
- *Start with a weekend campaign three weeks*

out from the event
- Run Wed-Sun two weeks out from the event
- Run every day the week of the event
By the time the event arrived, the market was ripe with anticipation.

3) Create a sense of urgency. This was the biggest lesson I learned from Aaron, and it's best told by this story:

It was about the fourth year in a row that Aaron and I had been working together and we'd developed a very good relationship. On Thursday, a day before his first show of the weekend, Aaron was driving into town. As soon as he got into range of our signal, he tuned into our radio station. Within an hour he heard one of his commercials. That's when all hell broke loose. He called me in a panic. "You're running the wrong commercial!" he screamed.

I was horrified. Instead of running the "week of" spot that said "this weekend," we were running the spot that gave the calendar date of the event. From my perspective, it was no big deal, the dates were correct. But from the promoter's perspective, it made all the difference in the world. So much so, that he bought every available piece of inventory we had left to ensure the success of his event.

I knew from his actions how important it was to him to have that sense of urgency. This guy knew how to sell tickets, and if it mattered that much to him that the spot say, "this weekend" or "tomorrow," then it must be important. Sure, it's a little extra work to create updates, but the payoff is worth it.

Working with Aaron helped me to become a better marketer. I'll never misjudge the value of timeliness and sense of urgency. I can't help but shutter in disgust now when I see an ad for a sale or event that is anything less than urgent. I'm talking about the ads that say, "This Friday, Saturday, and Sunday.." and it's already Sunday afternoon!

The formula still works...

- **Pick your best advertising vehicles, be they traditional and/or digital, and dominate**
- **Concentrate into fewer days for greater impact**
- **Make sure to create a sense of urgency!**

Follow these simple rules and get more out of your event advertising.

CHAPTER 25

FIVE LESSONS ON HOW TO SELL CONSUMERS FROM THE HOME SHOPPING NETWORK

Have you ever tuned in to the Home Shopping Network just to marvel at the pitches? Do you watch QVC and take notes? Maybe you should. At $10 billion a year in sales between QVC, HSN and ShopNBC, there's some serious retail going on!

Here are the Top 5 lessons I've learned from the shopping networks on how to advertise product...

1) Exclusivity. Consumers want to be first to own the latest, hottest, coolest products. Much of what the shopping networks offer are exclusive products or early releases. Their customers are even referred to as "Members."

Do you have the latest and greatest? Can you advertise something that only you can offer? Do you have a special loyalty program or membership club? Can you do special Invitation Only sales?

2) LTO (Limited Time Offer). Everything offered on the shopping networks has a deadline. Act now! Buy now! This offer goes away for good in 47 minutes!

To create a sense of urgency, you must have an offer with a deadline. Have you noticed how more and more retailers are using the shorter sale technique. Concepts like "Early Bird Specials" and "The Midnight Madness Sale" reward shoppers for taking advantage of short window opportunities.

3) Big Discounts. BOGO's, huge percent off sales, special discounts on top of discounts.

The standard 20%, 30%, even 40% off doesn't cut it anymore, unless it's off the already discounted price! Today, consumers are looking for the deal they can't pass up.

4) Easy Pay. This goes beyond "3 Easy Payments." Shopping networks have technology that allows viewers to buy product with a click of the remote. QVC has a mobile app you can download.

How are you making it easy for customers to do business with you?

5) No Risk. Money-back guarantees eliminate any risk to the sale.

How are you eliminating risk for your customers?

Home shopping networks, auction sites, and online retail are changing the way consumers think about the buying process. Take the lead from these nontraditional entities and make sure your business can compete.

CHAPTER 26

THE BIGGEST MISTAKE MOST LOCAL ADVERTISERS MAKE...

Diversify. Spread it around. Reduce the risk. It's a long-standing, well-regarded strategy in the business world. "You need to diversify your portfolio to protect yourself," would be typical advice you might hear from a financial planner. An ad agency might recommend a "media mix" to cover all your bases. Sounds smart. Unfortunately, when it comes to local advertising, it's the biggest mistake most local advertisers make!

Most local advertisers try to be in way too many places than their budget will allow.

When it comes to where to invest their advertising budget, most local advertisers execute the "little bit here, little bit there" mentality. Most local advertisers don't have enough confidence in any specific medium to commit to a dominant presence, so instead, they dabble in lots of different advertising vehicles and end up with zero presence

133

in any of them.

Our recommendation? Get focused in fewer places. Identify the outlets where you're currently investing advertising dollars that aren't delivering the results you demand, and stop spending with those partners! Recapture those precious advertising dollars and move them to those few advertising outlets you know are working. Identify those few advertising outlets that are highly targeted to your core, that you already know are working, and dominate there.

I've had to tell many local advertisers over the years, "you don't have the budget to be effective in all the places you're in!" And, if you're not sure whether it's working for you, why spend there? Jim Doyle & Associates has been built on recommending that advertisers redirect their ineffective ad dollars over to those media outlets that are targeted and are already working. We've helped thousands of local advertisers increase their advertising results without increasing their advertising budget. As my colleague, Senior Marketing Consultant, David Melville, simply, yet brilliantly puts it, "Find out what works, then do more of it."

But we see it all the time—advertisers who insist on spreading it around, taking little bits of their budget and trying every little advertising opportunity. It's typically driven out of fear that they'll "miss somebody." Usually the biggest offenders are those with the smallest budgets, and those are the advertisers who can least afford to do so. For years, Jim Doyle has said, "The scarcer your resources, the narrower your focus should be." Those businesses with little to invest in advertising need to be more discreet with where they spend.

To be more effective, learn to concentrate your ad spend. Concentrate into fewer places. Concentrate into fewer weeks. Concentrate into fewer days. Concentrate into fewer dayparts. Concentrate into fewer programs.

As a local advertiser, you're probably in way more places than you think. I've asked many local advertisers, "So, how many different places are you spending?" I typically hear an answer like this, "Oh, I dunno, five or six, I guess. Maybe seven..." Then, when I run down my exhaustive list of absolutely every place imaginable a local advertiser could spend money, we find out that they're in sixteen different places! It counts if you're spending money in the church bulletin. It counts if you're spending money in the high school yearbook. It counts if you're sponsoring a booth at the health fair. Lifestyle magazines, radio, broadcast television, cable television, Google Adwords, Angie's List, Yellow Pages, Facebook, direct mail, bus sides, billboards, SEO, SEM, newspaper, sandwich boards, county fairs—it all counts! A dollar spent on a less effective avenue is a dollar you could be spending to build on the other dollars on the ones that work!

Practice the law of sacrifice, which says, "In order to attain something you believe is of greater value, you must give up something you believe is of lesser value." Force yourself to identify what's working and what isn't, and give up those outlets that are not working. Practicing the Law of Sacrifice becomes much easier when you know what's working for you, and you're better able to know what's working for you when you stop branding and create a spectacular offer.

Hopefully, you agree that advertising builds over time. There's a saying: "The last dollar in is the best dollar spent." This means that once you identify those few advertising vehicles that work for you, and you commit to dominating those vehicles, each new dollar you add reaps the momentum of the other dollars already invested there. Each new dollar in has the momentum of the other dollars working for it, so the next dollar works better, and the next dollar works even better, and so on.

It's kind of like being on the treadmill. Imagine if you woke up this morning and said, "I'm gonna do a half hour today," and you got on the treadmill and away you went. Then you get to your thirtieth minute and say, "Whew, that was a good workout." You know what? If you could squeeze five more minutes out of yourself right then and there, that would be the best five minutes you spent on the treadmill. Your heart rate is up and you'll burn more calories in that five minutes than the first five, and the five minutes after that will be an even better increment, and so on.

"The last dollar in is the best dollar spent." It's that momentum that will give you the snowball effect in advertising we're all after—the "oh my gosh, I see you all over the place!" response. The way to achieve "I see you all over the place" is not by putting a little bit here and a little bit there. It is, in fact, by advertising in fewer places with super high frequency.

I once met with a dominant player in the funeral category in the Midwest. They had 11 locations and did 33% market share! Television was a good part of their total advertising budget and they were using 4 local broadcast stations in the market. After years of experience, they decided broadcast television delivered the best return on their advertising investment, so that's where they allocated the bulk of their advertising budget. Their budget was healthy, but I felt it wasn't big enough to justify using all four broadcast stations. Even with a healthy budget, by choosing to use four stations, they were spreading it too thin. I knew that by concentrating into fewer stations, they'd increase their frequency, thus increasing the effectiveness of their ad spend.

To support my position, I compared a schedule using 15 commercials a week over the 4 stations (total of 60 commercials) to a schedule running 30 commercials a week on just two stations (again, a total of 60 commercials). As expected, the frequency went up dramatically. And, because we narrowed to the two most targeted stations of the four, the reach went up dramatically as well! It was a powerful statement to the client—same number of commercials over fewer stations made the schedule far more effective.

Stop spreading it around.

CHAPTER 27

DID IT WORK?

One of the critical steps in executing any advertising/marketing campaign is to make sure you determine, in advance, what has to happen in order for the campaign to be considered a success. Here are two quick, true stories:

1) I met with a healthcare client who was considering an aggressive campaign for the coming year. The client said that he'd tried TV in September by sponsoring the National Cancer Awareness event. He told me that they typically see 320 new patients each month. In September, they saw their average 320 new patients, but in October, after the September campaign, they saw 400 new patients. In November, with no more advertising, they went back to 320 new patients.

So, my thought was, *that says it all!* The September advertising drove a huge 25% increase in new patients in the month immediately following the campaign.

139

But, that's not how the client saw it. His response to me was, "Well, I'm sure the advertising didn't hurt, but I really don't know how much it affected our business..."

Didn't hurt? Didn't hurt! By my standards, that advertising drove a 25% increase.

2) I followed up on an annual campaign on which I had consulted. It was for a John Deere dealer in the Midwest. A year earlier, he'd told me that he wanted to focus on used farm equipment. I suggested that he only focus the creative on used equipment with a call to action of driving traffic to his website, where he had all of his inventory.

At the annual review, the dealer felt like the campaign hadn't worked. He said no one came in and bought one of the advertised pieces of equipment. When I asked about his site traffic, he said he didn't know what his website traffic was (he didn't know how to check that). So, he determined the campaign didn't work.

Oh, by the way, sales were UP FOR THE YEAR!

These are two real examples of advertisers who truly didn't believe the advertising had worked, yet clearly, very good things happened to their businesses.

With a stronger emphasis on Return on Investment (ROI), you need to establish, prior to any advertising you do, what has to happen in order to consider the advertising campaign a success. If you spend money, run a campaign and haven't determined your goals upfront, you're setting yourself up for failure, even if, by realistic standards, it worked.

In our first example, it's my bet that if the healthcare advertiser had been asked by the rep, "How many new patients will you have to see in October to consider this investment worthwhile?" his answer wouldn't have even been as high as 400. Yet, even though the campaign delivered that number, he still wasn't ready to give the advertising campaign the credit it deserved.

In the second example, when you use "driving traffic to my website" as a call to action, you must benchmark site traffic, in advance, if you want to have any judgment of success.

Sometimes I'll hear, "No one came into my store." This is not a legitimate excuse if the campaign's call to action was to "go to the website." We really need to understand that driving traffic to a website is what we ask almost all of today's campaigns to do. If you have a weak non-mobile-friendly website and don't monitor your traffic, you're setting yourself up for failure. In fact, I've encountered example after example of campaigns that delivered website traffic increases that didn't translate to an increase in sales, and consequently the advertiser felt the campaign failed. Folks, you don't have an advertising problem, you have a conversion problem! The advertising worked, it did its job, it brought eyeballs to your front door (albeit virtual). If that traffic didn't convert, it's because the visitor didn't get what they wanted at your site!

If you want to make sure your advertising dollars are doing what you expect them to, make sure you've thought about what success means to you. Ask yourself, "What needs to happen in order for this to be a success?" And, make sure your rep knows what your expectations are as well.

And, of course, establishing goals upfront helps you manage expectations. Make sure you don't run a campaign without asking, "What will need to happen in order to consider this a success?" And be specific as you can.

CHAPTER 28

DON'T CHOP DOWN YOUR TREES BEFORE THEY'VE HAD A CHANCE TO GROW!

One of the most common mistakes we see local advertisers make is changing creative too frequently. Advertisers get bored with their creative and insist on making a change. Often, they've gone through a tedious, if not intense, creative process involving drafts and revisions of a script or concept, followed by actual production to get the piece of creative made, more revisions, and approvals from decision makers. So, by the time a final piece of creative is ready to be delivered to the market, they're totally sick of it! It's no wonder that while the campaign is still in its infancy, they're dreaming about what they can do next.

Compound that with their sales team and other influencers who might have been in on the process and want immediate results, or who just want a change because they've also been highly exposed to the creative and are bored. The result is the advertiser makes the mistake of pulling the plug

143

right when that campaign is hitting critical frequency with their prospects and is ready to explode!

Sometimes, advertisers want change just for the sake of change! It was a December morning when we received an email from a local television account executive who wrote, "The granite countertop client you helped me with this year is up for renewal. They loved the 'rock bottom pricing' idea you guys came up with. They're up over 20% this year. I'm preparing my proposal for next year's annual, what new creative ideas do you have for me?"

Here's a winning idea: keep running the current campaign!!

Why would you need a new idea? They're up over 20%! Keep it going!

More often than not, however, we get 911 calls from advertisers and account executives who say something like, "We've been running for about a month and we're not seeing the results yet. What other ideas do you have?" In almost all of those cases, they haven't given their creative a chance to work. Most campaigns go through a response phase before they hit their results stride. Response phase is, "My neighbor says he sees my ad." Results phase is, "We just had our best weekend of the year." Getting to the results phase depends on numerous factors, including the strength of the offer, the urgency of the deadline, current economic conditions, even weather!

I'm not saying you shouldn't keep your ad fresh. For most advertisers, however, their definition of "fresh" is wholesale change—a completely new concept. New look, new approach, new style, new message. That's cutting down your trees before they've had a chance to grow and planting new seeds that will need time to take root. It's okay to freshen your ad by selecting a new product to feature, highlighting a seasonal change or updating your testimonials. But keep everything else as consistent as possible.

Here are the things to keep consistent in your creative:

- *The spokesperson*
- *The color scheme*
- *The font*
- *The music*
- *The tone*
- *The tempo*
- *The slogan*
- *The intro*
- *The outcue*

The goal is that over time, the consumer will recognize the creative as your commercial just by the look and feel, regardless of the specific content.

Keep as much of the ad as consistent as you can, for as long as you can, and don't chop down your trees before they've had a chance to grow!

Chapter 29

BEAT THE BUYING CYCLE

Another common question we hear from local advertisers, is "How long should I run?" That's a very legitimate question that any budget-conscious local advertiser would pose. Every local advertiser would love to be present, out there "running" some type of advertising 24/7/365. The problem is, it costs money to be on radio, television, billboards, Facebook, direct mail, whichever medium works best for you, all the time, and most local advertisers can't (or don't) budget for such. And, in fact, some highly seasonal businesses shouldn't!

I learned a ton about local advertising from working with a regional formal wear company in upstate New York that spent 100% of their advertising budget each year from January through April. Proms and weddings drive their business, so they'd kick off each year by sponsoring the biggest bridal show in town in January, and they'd follow up with aggressive advertising straight through prom season. Each year they'd work hard to come up with some amazing offer—FREE tux for the groom, $49 prom rentals—and they'd hammer it. Post wedding and prom season, they'd go dark with their advertising until the next year. Of course, they were open twelve months a year. If you needed a tux to attend a black tie event in September, they were your go-to formal wear store... because they had created that file in your mind through their dominant campaign during their peak season. By the way, today you can find Tuxedo Junction locations in 18 states from New York to California!

But, let's talk about the non-seasonal, non-sale-oriented advertiser, on a limited budget, who'd like to invest in advertising wisely. Every media rep who calls on you would love you to sign an annual agreement, but sometimes that's just not a reality. What do you do when you want to do business with a media partner and you want to execute a campaign, but you're just not ready to commit to the annual? How long should you run?

First off, let me say that if your inclination is to "try it for a month," save your money. That's not how advertising works. Trying anything for a month is a recipe for failure. One month or two months is not a fair enough opportunity for any medium to prove its worthiness. I spent a career listening to local advertisers tell me, "I tried it once, it doesn't work." If all you do is "try" different media on a month to month basis, with no consistency, no strategy, no plan, you'll get the results you deserve. None.

Which brings us back to "so how long should I run?" It's a simple question that requires a complex answer. Part of my answer would be, "As long as your budget will allow." Part of my answer would be, "As long as it's working." And a big part of my answer would be, "Long enough to beat your buying cycle."

Every business has a buying cycle—the average amount of time it takes a potential customer, client or patient to go from "I'm interested" to "Okay, I'll do it." Every business decision maker should have a good handle on their prospects' typical buying cycle. Today, buying cycles can be called things like "path to purchase" or "purchase funnel," and include pre-defined stages like awareness, research, consideration, intent, negotiation, purchase, and even post-purchase.

Certain categories have lengthy buying cycles such as auto dealerships, home improvement, cosmetic enhancement. Some categories have relatively short buying cycles like restaurants and retail. Typically, the larger the investment, the longer the buying cycle. It stands to reason that more research and consideration go into making major purchases. If you're in a "major purchase" category, my advice is to make sure to beat your buying cycle. Run your advertising campaign at least long enough to carry a prospect through your business's entire buying process. Running campaigns shorter than the length of time it takes someone to make a purchase decision is unfinished business!

Here's when this became apparent to me. I was the Director of Sales for an Internet development company in the early 2000's. We were a company that would build, host, and market websites. It was still the early adopter/early majority stage of Internet development, meaning there were plenty of businesses that hadn't yet embraced the Web with a strong online presence. I had had the position about two years, and at that point, had determined that our typical buying cycle was around 90 days. After two years of managing our sales efforts, I could deduce that it took about 90 days for a typical business decision maker to go from, "We'd better get a decent website" to "Here's a check, start development."

Our company was a good, strong player locally and we decided it was time to do some advertising. The owner of the company came to my office and said, "Tom, you're our resident marketing expert, you're in charge of our advertising."

This was a growing, successful company of about thirty employees at the time. We were riding the wave of explosive Internet development. The category was still in its infancy. There were no rules, no manuals, and we were just kind of making it up as we went along. But we were still a private business that didn't enjoy any angel investing, so our budgets weren't unlimited. I knew the advertising money entrusted to me was real money that could have just as easily gone into a new hire or new equipment. I took my advertising responsibility very seriously.

I decided we would use local television news to reach our market's local business decision makers. I decided we'd run testimonials from our best clients to demonstrate our capabilities.* One of my more important decisions was to determine how long I should run the campaign based on my budget restrictions. That's when it struck me. If it takes our typical prospect about 90 days to decide on an Internet development partner, then it made total sense to me that I needed to run our campaign at least 90 days. I felt we needed to be there every step of the way, and that running any shorter than 90 days would leave money on the table.

I knew to maximize our budget, we had to beat our buying cycle.

The campaign performed as I expected. Within the first week of the schedule, I came home from work one night and my wife said, "Hey! I just saw you guys on TV!" The next week I was at a local business function and a couple of people said, "Hey, I see you guys are doing some television. Good for you." Finally, about three or four weeks into the campaign, the phone rang in my office and the person on the other end said, "My name is Joe. I own Victor Precision Manufacturing. I've been seeing your ads. I'd like to talk to you guys about building us a new website." From response to results.

As the weeks went on, our phone rang more frequently with qualified prospects who needed our help, and at the end of our schedule we really felt the advertising surge kicking in and we decided to extend our campaign.

*I did make one mistake with our creative. The testimonials we used in our initial commercial were from our "blue chip" clients. We wanted to brag about the big name businesses we worked with. It got back to us pretty quickly that we were missing wheelhouse opportunities because prospects who should have called us, weren't, because they thought they were too small for us! You only need to hear, "I thought you guys only worked with the big companies…" a few times before you react to correct that perception! We quickly changed our creative to include testimonials from businesses that were a more accurate representation of our bread-and-butter clients.

CHAPTER 30

"HOW'D YA HEAR ABOUT US?"

Another standard question I ask all of the local advertisers I meet with is, "Do you track your advertising?" Often times, I'll get a very confident response, "Oh yeah! We track everything." That leads me to ask, "How do you track?" Which elicits the scary answer, "We ask everybody who walks in." Or, "We ask everybody who calls in."

I dig deeper. "What do you ask them?"

"How'd ya hear about us?" is the reply.

Okay, let's stop right there. If "how'd ya hear about us?" is your advertising tracking device, you are in big trouble! HYHAU is not only a flawed tracking system, it potentially does more damage than good!

Instead of asking HYHAU, you might as well ask every new prospect who walks in, "What'd ya have for breakfast yesterday?" because they don't know the answer to that question either. The data is almost as accurate!

In all seriousness, I would never be so bold as to tell you NOT to ask your customers, "How'd ya hear about us?" or "What brought you in today?" But, please be careful with the answers you receive. The reason is simple. Most people have no idea how they heard about you or what brought them in! That's not their responsibility. They don't care whether they heard about you on television, their smartphone, Facebook or at a cocktail party. Nor *should* they care. All that matters to them is that they have engaged your business, and that's what should matter most to you at that time.

Here's the real potential danger. Once you ask HYHAU (or WBYIT), the customer feels compelled to give you an answer... and they really don't know. So, now you're collecting bogus information! If you're a local business that aggressively trains all of your frontliners to ask HYHAU or WBYIT so you can track the effectiveness of your advertising and make decisions moving forward, I urge you to reconsider that strategy.

I bet that sometime in your business life, if HYHAU is your advertising tracking system, you've heard a response that you know full well is incorrect. At least once, if not many times, you've heard someone reply, "Oh, I heard you this morning on the Q101 Morning Zoo! It's the only thing I listen to!" And you know you've never, ever, ever spent a penny on that radio station. But they insist.

Here's the good news. Today, almost all initial contact is made via your website. Your website is your new front door, and the beauty of our digital tools is that they're completely trackable. Your Google analytics can tell you who came to your front door, how they got there, how long they stayed inside, where they wandered, and where they exited.

But there's still a danger in deciphering the data. Here's my digital HYHAU/WBYIT horror story...

I was meeting with a car dealership in a midsized market in the West. It was a nice dealership that featured Volvo and a few other import lines. The dealer brought his future son-in-law to the meeting, as the son-in-law had recently taken over all the advertising for the dealership. At the beginning of the meeting the son-in-law was quick to inform me that they would soon be cancelling all of their traditional advertising—no more television, no more radio, no more direct mail, no more billboards. He told me that instead, they'd be reinvesting that money into better signage at the storefront.

I took a few seconds to process what I had just heard. Did this guy really just tell me his television campaign was being trumped for more balloons? His radio was being replaced by an air dancer?

"What's driving this decision?" I had to ask.

His explanation: "We've installed new dealer

management software and we make all of our salespeople ask, 'What brought you in today?' and the number one answer logged in by our salespeople, by far, is, 'Just driving by...' So we're pulling our advertising and spending that money on our storefront."

Well then, if that's what the data says...

That Friday night, while flying back home, I became engaged in a friendly conversation with the passenger sitting next to me. We exchanged the typical pleasantries, and after some conversation, I asked her, what she did for a living. She replied, "Oh, I work for a company called Reynolds and Reynolds," fully anticipating that I'd have no idea who that was.

"Oh, the automotive software company?" I said.

She was surprised. "You know about Reynolds and Reynolds?"

"Yeah. I used to work for an Internet development company and we'd have to integrate with Reynolds and Reynolds for the backend of our car dealer websites." I said, quite proudly, "So, what do you do for Reynolds and Reynolds?"

"I'm a trainer. I go into the dealerships and help them learn and use our system."

"Hmmmm... do you ever get into the showroom and interact with the salespeople?" I asked.

"Oh yeah, all the time," she replied.

"Okay, so let me ask you a question. Does your

software have anything like a lead tracking component to it?"

"Most definitely," my new friend responded. "It's a big part of what we pitch to our dealers. In fact, salespeople can't even log in an up (car slang for customer) until they fill in the 'what brought you in today' field."

"And how does that field work?" I pressed.

"It's a drop-down menu."

"And what's the first choice on the drop-down menu?"

"Just driving by."

Enlightenment at 30,000 feet!

"What brought you in today?" "So, how'd you hear about us?" are NOT systematic ways to make advertising decisions, regardless of how you received the information. And their cousin, "Well, nobody came right out and said they saw the ad... (but business is up 12%)..." is just as dangerous!

CHAPTER 31

THREE TIPS MOVING FORWARD

I said in the "Introduction" that writing a book about advertising is "dangerous" because it's constantly changing. New technologies regularly make today's hot tool next week's old news. I will, however, identify three "trends" that will continue to be critically important to the local advertiser, regardless of the hot technique or tool of the day.

The first is video. Not only is video not going away, it's role is increasing. Today, every person with a smartphone is a broadcaster with the ability to capture video and instantly share it with the world. As an advertiser, in the past you may have thought of video in terms of :30 second, highly produced units. Today, video helps to market your business on Facebook, on a YouTube channel for your business, on your own website, and in countless other opportunities. In the fall of 2014, it was Mark Zuckerberg at a Facebook community town hall meeting who said, "In five years, most of

Facebook will be video." And it didn't take that long for us to see the proliferation of video in our Facebook feeds.

So, are you using video to market your business? If I visited your website, would I find video? I'm not talking about, "Welcome to my homepage..." videos. I'm talking about understanding your most highly trafficked pages and having good, compelling, well-produced video, with a value proposition. Are you putting a high priority on capturing and creating video to help market your business? When it comes to video, remember, it's less about promotion and hype, and more about creating helpful video that delivers usable content. So, rather than creating and posting long-winded, "Here's why we're the greatest thing since sliced bread..." videos, you'd be much better served by creating educational, helpful, "Here are the five things you need to know about this category..." videos. That's what consumers want to view.

Video only needs a screen, and we all have a screen in our hands, which is a perfect segue to my second trend, mobile. It's hard to even call mobile a "trend" anymore. It's solidified itself into the fabric of the American consumer, yet it continues to grow.

Mobile has surpassed the desktop as the screen that consumers interact on most. In fact, it was in 2015 that Google changed its algorithm because of the mobile device. Now, Google changes their algorithm regularly (500 to 600 times a year according to a Google search!). They just don't tell us about them. However, in 2015, they warned us about their algorithm change. They were calling it "Mobilegeddon!" In early 2015, Google publicized that on April 21, 2015, if your website did not meet Google's mobile-optimized standards, you would be punished in the rankings! Today, it's imperative that your website be mobile-optimized. When more searches happen on a mobile device than a desktop, when more than half of all Internet traffic happens on a mobile device, you'd better make sure you're well-represented on mobile.

As an advertiser, consider this—nothing can bring you closer to your customer than mobile... NOTHING. Let that sink in. Nothing puts you closer to your client, your customer, your prospect, your patient, however you define them, than the mobile device, which is always within their arms reach 24/7/365. Your advertising can reach your prospect anytime, day or night, on their mobile device, no matter where they are, including when they're standing in front of your business! GPS and beacon technology allow local advertisers the opportunity to deliver messages and capture habits and patterns right down to your front curb. It's the mobile device that allows a prospect to search your company, call you directly with one tap of their finger, get turn-by-turn directions to your door or simply place an order, all from the palm of their hand.

As we said in an earlier chapter, today when an ad works, people pick up a device. Well, you'd better have a "pick up a device" strategy.

Finally, as new and exciting tools are constantly being introduced, don't overlook the value of email. While email may be "long in the tooth" as far as digital marketing goes, it can still be an extremely effective and cost efficient tool. There's still tremendous value in a strong email database.

I was doing yardwork one weekend when my pest control provider came for a regular service call. Geovanni pulled up while I was out mowing the lawn. After some friendly chit-chat, Geo went to work. When he was done, he said, "We won't be leaving the hand-written report door hangers anymore. Would you please update your email address with me and we'll be sending reports out via email from now on."

Okay, I'll take email over paper any day, so I gladly obliged. It wasn't until later that I realized my pest control company can use my email to query an outside service to create a complete customer identity and market back to me with things like loyalty programs, email newsletters, Facebook campaigns, and event calendars.

A strong email database is the foundation of

good equity mining—tapping into your current customer base. As a local advertiser, you're constantly thinking of the best way to drive new customers, as well you should. But if you're diligent at building and maintaining a solid database of current customer emails, you're sitting atop a gold mine of opportunity. Granted, it's a never-ending battle, but you need to be constantly looking to capture email addresses as both a customer acquisition and retention tool.

Chapter 32

BEWARE THE LAST MILE

In the tech world, it's known as "the last mile," and it refers to that metaphoric final distance from the provider to the end user. What it means is that your Internet provider may have huge fiber optics in place, but your home's Internet service is only as good as bandwidth that can pass through the last mile of your network. The last mile is notorious for being "the bottleneck" to better performance.

In advertising, there's a last mile of which you, the local advertiser, must be aware. For all the hard work and thought power put into a typical campaign, it can all get derailed at the last mile— the initial point of contact between you and your prospect. All too often, I see local advertisers investing precious advertising dollars, only to risk it all with a staff or website that is unprepared, uninformed or simply disinterested in handling the results of the advertising. Many a time, upon hearing from an advertiser, "It's not working," I've secret-shopped the client, only to discover that the breakdown is in their ability to convert a lead.

These breakdowns go beyond the simple, yet inexcusable, instance of a frontline employee who is plain unaware of an ad campaign. I'm talking about advertisers who have broken systems. For example, have you ever been prompted by an ad to visit a website, only to be forced to dig deep in the site to find the very thing advertised? It's incredibly frustrating, and worse yet, most won't even bother searching. If the call to action in your ad is to visit a website, you'd better make it as easy as possible to find what was advertised. If you're a dentist who's going to plant your flag in sedation dentistry and your call to action in your ad is to visit your website, at the very least I'd better see a great big call out button on your homepage that says, "click here to learn more about our sedation techniques." An even better strategy would be to drive me to a landing page that's specifically built to support the advertising creative—same look, same feel, same language, same offer strategy. In fact, buy the domain, "mytownsedationdentist-.com," use it as the call to action in your advertising, and build a supporting landing page that is singularly dedicated to sedation dentistry. Have a "click here" button on the landing page that's the next step in your conversion strategy, e.g., download my whitepaper, sign up for my seminar, print a coupon for a FREE first visit...

I say it to advertisers all the time, "You don't have an advertising problem, you have a conversion problem!" Their advertising worked, it prompted prospects to take action. Where the breach occurs is in the last mile.

Healthcare advertisers are notorious for giving away too much information on the initial call. The intake specialist (the person who answers the phone) will take as much time as the prospect wants to answer questions about the practice, the doctor, the procedure. The only goal of the intake specialist should be to secure the appointment! A good intake specialist will know when the campaign is scheduled to run, right down to the minute. A good intake specialist will be fully aware of the creative that's running, especially the call to action and offer. And a good intake specialist answers questions by saying, "The doctor will cover all of that on your initial visit. We have an opening Thursday at 9am. Can I schedule you there?"

I have a friend who works for a television station in the Midwest. Her name is Sue. Every client she works with goes through a rigorous "Last Mile" process before she allows their campaign to begin. She finds out what their phone number is, is it easy to remember, she'll help secure a special vanity number for advertising purposes. Sue finds out how many phone lines her clients have, as one or two may not be enough. She strategizes what happens if all lines are busy. What's the "on hold" message? Can they leave a message? Will prospects receive a call back within the hour?

Before she'll begin a campaign, Sue uncovers what day of the week most people will call and what time of the day most people will call. Sue will prepare a lunch-hour strategy. She'll prepare an after-hours strategy. In one healthcare client case, each new patient represented thousands in revenue, so Sue set up an "on call" schedule for the staff with a forwarding line for after-hours inquiries. She didn't want to risk even one inquiry not speaking to a live person.

After Sue crafts your creative script, she crafts a second script—one for your staff to use when the calls start coming in! She calls it a "rough draft" because she wants the client's staff to use their own words so they feel comfortable with the verbiage. The script will come complete with an "if this, then that" tree that specifically details the appropriate answers to all of the common questions.

Our company has been recommending advertiser "Launch Parties" for years. Our suggestion is that advertisers kick off their campaigns with fanfare and celebration to rev up their team and prepare them for increased results.

Invite your advertising partner to come in and address your team. Show the creative, talk about the strategy, detail the "Last Mile" responsibilities. As a business owner, you know the sizable investment you're making in your advertising budget. You also know it's called an "investment" because you're expecting a return on it. Get credit with your staff on the investment your making. You don't need to tell them specific amounts, but do let them know that you're investing serious money to keep business healthy and keep them happily employed.

Foxy's

(If you are easily offended, you might want to skip this chapter.)

For more than three decades, I've helped local advertisers earn better results. It's basically all I've ever done in my professional life. Obviously, it took years to learn all the lessons in this book, and my real-life advertising "Ph.D" really kicked in when I started traveling the country in 2005. But I've always had a pretty good handle on what works and what doesn't for local advertisers. So, I'm going to reach way back to the early days of my media career to share a story that pretty much sums up so much of what I've written in this book.

It was the early 1990's and I was an account executive for a classic rock radio station in Rochester, NY. The station was a dominant, powerhouse player, featuring the city's big morning show personality. At the time, I was a member of a local "tip club," a group of non-competing business folks who met weekly to share leads, tips, and local insights. At one particular tip club meeting, it was shared that a shuttered, suburban night club in a tiny suburb called Scottville would soon be re-opening under new ownership as... a strip club.

That got my attention. Not because I enjoy strip clubs. I don't. In fact, I find them rather depressing. However, as an account executive for a classic rock radio station, I actually handled a couple of different "gentlemen's clubs" in the Rochester market. I visited each one once a week to pick up a check and get the copy points for the next week's commercials. And, by copy points, I mean who the national feature act was going to be. Basically, every week a different former Playboy or Penthouse model would appear, and her "resume" would drive the commercial copy. We insisted the clubs pay cash-in-advance and we'd only run their commercials between 10pm and 2am. It wasn't a huge category for us, but we had a few that advertised regularly.

Upon learning of this new club that would be opening soon, I made the forty-minute drive to the outskirts of town to investigate. Sure enough, when I arrived, I walked into a flurry of activity that signaled a Grand Opening was imminent. I asked for the owner and was introduced to brothers, Mike and Joe.

"I'm Tom Ray with WCMF radio," was all I said.

"Ah yeah, the Brother Wease station!" they

replied, referencing our popular morning show DJ. "Yeah, we're gonna want to do some advertising with you guys!" Music to my ears.

I sat for a few minutes with Mike and Joe to learn about their plan for "Foxy's." At one point I said, "So, I assume you'll be bringing in national features each week?"

Their answer surprised me. "No, no," the brothers replied. "We're not gonna mess with none of that. Only local girls here."

Local girls only at a strip club that's on the outskirts of town, with no national features to drive attendance. That's about as close to "three stikes, yer out!" as it gets in the competitive world of local strip clubs.

I remember sitting that evening at the keyboard of my Packard Bell thinking, *How the hell am I going to get guys to this joint!?* The idea of driving past cows and pastures to see local girls didn't seem like a formula for "gentlemen's club" success to me. In fact, about the only reason I could think of that would motivate a bunch of guys to make that drive would be maybe, if by chance, they might happen to know one of the dancers.

Wait! That's it!

Foxy's... where girls from your neighborhood... strip!

So it was born. I was so excited that I drove back out to the club the very next day to share my idea. The brothers loved it.

The week of the grand opening, I grabbed a microphone and the Marantz recorder from our production department and set up shop at the club. The brothers literally cleaned out a broom closet for me, and one by one, the dancers would come in and I'd have them record a line or two. Each girl would give her name, her high school class and a brief sell line.

"I'm Lacey, Fairport High class of '89. Catch me in the flesh, tonight at Foxy's..."

"I'm Tabitha from Gates Central, class of '91. I'll make your dreams come true, tonight at Foxy's."

Throw in a drink special and the announcer outcue was always the same, "Foxy's... where girls from your neighborhood... strrrrrrrippppppp!"

The campaign began with a spot an hour, 10pm to 2am, Wednesday through Saturday. It was an instant success. The very first week it aired, guys were showing up with their high school yearbooks. Calls were coming in every day asking if "Ashley from Spencerport High is going to be there tonight?"

Yes, the names were made up, none of the girls wanted to use their real names. In fact, I only did the broom closet recording session a few times. I realized pretty quickly that sexy on stage didn't always equate to a sexy voice! I ended up using female staffers from around the radio station for future campaigns.

I knew the campaign was a hit when I was sitting in a sports bar watching football about three months into the campaign, and I overhead a bunch of guys talking. One of them said, "Hey, have any of you guys been to that new strip club yet?" And one shouted, "You mean Foxy's, where girls from your neighborhood strrrripppp!"

I wanted to turn around and say, "I wrote that!"

I hope this story didn't turn you off. I actually wrestled with including it in the book. But it's a great example of so much of what I know works in local advertising.

- **Target the right audience, focusing on the core.** Late night classic rock radio listeners.
- **Deliver the right message, focusing on your "one thing."** Local girls.
- **Do it with super high frequency.** A spot an hour.

I firmly believe this campaign would work today. The medium might be different. There would certainly be a digital component (imagine getting geo-targeted with an ad on your mobile device). But the elements of proper target, right message, and frequency still apply. With Foxy's, we certainly created a file in the minds of the consumers. In fact, we moved them from a cluttered file by creating one only they could own.

ABOUT THE AUTHOR

Tom Ray is Executive Vice President of Jim Doyle & Associates. He has over 30 years of LOCAL media experience. From radio, to broadcast and cable television, to Internet development and marketing, Tom's diverse background gives him a unique perspective on driving results for the LOCAL advertiser.

For more than a decade, he has travelled the country, helping businesses discover what works and what doesn't in local advertising.

Tom is a member of the National Speakers Association and has achieved their highest designation of Certified Speaking Professional (CSP). He has been a featured speaker for the National Association of Broadcasters, at various State Broadcasters Association events, and has shared his advertising insights for thousands of local businesses in markets big and small across the US.

Here's what business owners around the country say about Tom's signature presentation, "The NEW Rules of LOCAL Advertising – Driving Results in a Four Screen World":

- *"The best seminar I've attended since leaving a Fortune 500 company 30 years ago!*
- *"Very good material—well presented—clear & powerful—well-timed for today's environment."*
- *"Highly instructive—everything presented was quite relative to me as a local businessperson."*
- *"Gave us a lot to think about—possibly helped to rethink our marketing."*
- *"Tom was incredibly charismatic and knowledgeable. The presentation brought up great questions and gave me some awesome new ideas."*
- *"I've sat through a lot of seminars and marketing courses and this was phenomenal!"*

Tom is a featured contributor to the Jim Doyle & Associates acclaimed learning platform, Doyle on Demand™.

EXPERIENCE
DOYLE ON DEMAND

The Television Industry's Premier
Sales Training Platform

Amulti-million dollar virtual interactive sales training platform, with 24/7 access via mobile, tablet, computer or any electronic device that has access to the Internet.

For the rookie seeking that first sale to sales veterans looking for new revenue highs to managers and leaders bent on building the best sales organizations in the industry, Doyle on Demand offers multiple interactive training courses and chapters designed to make you money and make you better.

TO FIND OUT HOW DOYLE ON DEMAND CAN HELP YOUR TEAM:

 Tour: www.doyleondemand.com
Email: info@jimdoyle.com
Call Us: 941-926-*SELL* (7355)

THE LEADERS EDGE
COACHING PROGRAM

L et's face it. Our business is getting more difficult and complex every day. Change is occurring at the speed of light and it's your job to develop strategies and tactics and, even more importantly, to motivate your team to capitalize on these changes and lead them to success.

But you can't do it alone! You need a leadership coach—more specifically, a PERSONAL leadership coach! THE LEADERS EDGE PROGRAM is just that... a comprehensive personal coaching program specifically designed for TV and Cable sales managers. If the *Engaged Management* series has made an impact on you, then you'll want to check out this ongoing, multi-formatted, real-world program that's guaranteed to help you become a stronger leader. And great sales organizations are the result of STRONG LEADERSHIP!

TO LEARN MORE ABOUT THE LEADERS EDGE COACHING PROGRAM:

 Visit: www.jimdoyle.com/store-2
Email: info@jimdoyle.com
Call Us: 941-926-*SELL* (7355)

CONTACTS

Tom Ray
Jim Doyle & Associates, Inc.
7711 Holiday Drive
Sarasota, FL 34231

941-926-7355
tom@jimdoyle.com
www.jimdoyle.com
www.doyleondemand.com

 @thomaseray

 /JimDoyleandAssociates

 /company/jim-doyle-&-associates

 /TVJimDoyle

52442136R00111

Made in the USA
Columbia, SC
03 March 2019